Alphonse Esquiros

Cornwall and Its Coasts

Alphonse Esquiros

Cornwall and Its Coasts

ISBN/EAN: 9783337016777

Printed in Europe, USA, Canada, Australia, Japan

Cover: Foto ©Andreas Hilbeck / pixelio.de

More available books at **www.hansebooks.com**

CORNWALL

AND ITS COASTS.

BY

ALPHONSE ESQUIROS,

AUTHOR OF "ENGLISH AT HOME," ETC.

LONDON:
CHAPMAN AND HALL, 193 PICCADILLY.
1865.

LONDON: PRINTED BY WILLIAM CLOWES AND SONS, STAMFORD STREET
AND CHARING CROSS.

CONTENTS.

CHAPTER I.

Why the English travel—Plymouth and the Tamar—Albert Bridge—Difference between Devon and Cornwall—Configuration of England—William Gilpin—Mistakes of old Geographers about the causes of the Temperature—Peculiar Climate of Cornwall—Mr. Were Foxe's Gardens—Perpetual Spring—Cottage Gardening Societies—Flowers and Bees—The Chough—Lostwithiel—Restormel Castle—The Harvest and the Mows—Farms and Farmers—Influence of Rocks and Climate upon House Building—The Inner Life of Rich Families—Home of the Labourers—Polytechnic Society—Falmouth—Opening of the Railway 1

CHAPTER II.

A Silver Mine—The English Mont St. Michel—The Phœnicians in Cornwall—The Jews and Marazion—Exterior of the Copper and Tin Mines—Carclaze—China Clay—Saint Austel—Submarine Mines—Botallack—Wherry Mine—Camborne and Redruth—Carn-Brea—Mining Speculations—The Adventurers—The Great Adit—Looe Pool, or the Red Lake—Length of the Ladders—Man-engine—Accidents peculiar to Miners—Pay Day—Sales by Auction—Education of the Miners—Their Manners—Coquetry of the Women—The Pack-man—Sunday in Cornwall—Philosophy of Dress 35

CHAPTER III.

Brixham—Present State of the Town and Port—The Fishing-boats—The Market—The Lords of the Manor—Home Missionaries—Fishermen's Wives—Nets—General Opinion about the Trawl—Clement Pine—Anne Perriam—Distress at Seaton—Difference between the Devon and Cornish Fisheries 78

CHAPTER IV.

Fabulous Origin of Helston—The Fiend in Cornish Legends—Tregeagle—The Furry—Cape Lizard—Appearance of the Celtic Race—The primitive Language of Cornwall—Traces of Spanish Origin—A Fisherman's Story—Queen Zenobia—Are the Inhabitants of Cornwall descended from the Phœnicians?—Lizard Fishery Cove—Kynance Cove—The Promontories and Rocks—The Caverns—The Devil's Frying-pan—Dolor Hugo—Composition of the Rocks—Serpentine—The Land's End—John Wesley and Turner—Architecture of the Rocks—Dr. Johnson—Sennen—The School—Shipwrecks—The First and Last Inn in England—The Three Kings 94

CHAPTER V.

Mount's Bay—Changes on the Coast—Newlyn and Mousehole—Appearance of these two Villages—The Pilchard, where does it come from?—Its Migrations—The Drift-net and the Seine—The Fishing Fleet—Method of Spreading the Nets—General Results of Drift-net Fishing—The Market—The Queen of the Fishwomen—The Curling—The Fish Cellar—Caprices of the Pilchard—A Fisherman's Home—A Voyage to Australia—Dolly Pentreath—Sunday in a Fishing Village—John Wesley—The Dissenters and the Church of England—Saint Ives—A lost Church—Mr. Bolitho's Cellars—Seine Fishing—The Huers—The Floating Prison—Produce of the Fishery—Moral Character of the Fishermen 125

CHAPTER VI.

General State of the English Coast—Shipwrecks—Exmouth—Devon and Cornwall Archery Company—The Coastguard Station—A Watering-place—The Life-boat House—The Bird and the Life-boat—Lionel Lukin and Mr. Greathead—James Beeching—The Margate Life-boat—The Samaritano—Theory of an Insubmersible Boat—The Air Chambers—Self-return—Discharge of the Water—A Life-boat at Sea—The Carriage—A Cornish Legend—The Life-boat Stations—An Heroic Schoolmaster—A Preacher's Remark—Character of the Cornish Coast—The Bells of Boscastle—Bude—Barometers—Admiral Fitzroy—The Rocket Apparatus 155

CHAPTER VII.

Origin of the Life-boat Society—Sir William Hillary—Decadence and Recovery of the System—A Fortunate Catastrophe—Character of the Donations—Their Motives—The Bude Haven Life-boat—Number of Persons Rescued since the Foundation of the Society—The Disaster at Scarborough in 1861—Medals and Honorary Certificates—James M'Millan—A Procession following a Life-boat—Receipts of the Society—The Officers and Secretary—Expenses of the Company—The Victories of Peace 190

CHAPTER VIII.

The Wreck of the 'Forfarshire'—Grace Horsley Darling—Eliza Byrne—Wreck of the 'Royal Charter'—Joseph Rogers—Saving a Fishing-boat on the Harboro' Sands—'The Countess of Lisburne'—A Cornish Fisherman aboard a Life-boat—A Struggle between Jealousy and Duty—Comparison between the Means of Rescue in France and England—How the Superiority of Modern Civilization over Ancient Countries is recognized 210

CHAPTER IX.

Antiquity of Lighthouses—Why they were neglected in the Middle Ages—Trinity House—Origin and History of this maritime Institution—Charter of Henry VIII.—Traces of a Catholic Institution—Deptford—Sayer's Court and John Evelyn—Peter the Great—St. Nicholas Church and the Duke of Wellington—Stepney and Sir Thomas Spert—Elder Brothers and younger Brothers—Honorary and active Members—Duties of the various Committees—James I. at Trinity House—Disastrous Consequences of Royal Interference—Advantages of the New System—The Board of Trade—The Northern Commissioners and the Ballast Board. 225

CHAPTER X.

Floating Lights—The Nore Light—Robert Hamblin—Geological Law determining the Existence of Light-vessels—The Goodwin Sands—The Scilly Isles—Science and Legends—The 'Maiden Bower'—An Officious Cicerone—General Appearance of the Isles—St. Mary's and Hugh Town—My Landlord's House—Two romantic Sisters—Sunday at St. Mary's—Manners of the Inhabitants—Maternity before Marriage—The Doctor, Policeman, and Garrison—The Cassiterides of the Greeks—Mr. Augustus Smith—Celtic Antiquities—Trade of the Scilly Men—Agriculture, Gardens and Farms—The Island Flora—The Building Mania . . 246

CHAPTER XI.

The Admiral's Grave—The Sharks—The Light-vessel at Seven Stones—Characteristics of a Light-vessel—The Chains—An escaped Convict—The Crews of the Light-ships—One Month ashore and two afloat—Insufficient Food—The Argand Lamp —Life of the Men aboard—A Bird Pie—Discipline—The Cost of a Light-vessel 268

CHAPTER XII.

Three Systems of Lighthouses—Plymouth Breakwater—Fog-Signals—The Bell and the Sea-gulls—The Story of Eddystone Lighthouse—Henry Winstanley—John Rudierd—The Lighthouse on Fire—Smeaton—A Tree of Stone—Exterior and Interior of Eddystone Lighthouse—Its Appearance during a Storm—The Lighthouse now kept by Three Men—Life of the Keepers—A Cobbler shut up through Hatred of Captivity—Longship's Lighthouse and the roaring Caverns—A silent Light-keeper—The Smalls and Whiteside—Danger of Starvation—The Double Stanners Light—Point of Honour among the Keepers—Bell Rock Lighthouse—Robert Stephenson—The Skerryvore Lighthouse—Alan Stephenson—Systems of Lighting—Authority and Liberty . . 280

CORNWALL AND ITS COASTS.

CHAPTER I.

WHY THE ENGLISH TRAVEL — PLYMOUTH AND THE TAMAR — ALBERT BRIDGE—DIFFERENCE BETWEEN DEVON AND CORNWALL—CONFIGURATION OF CORNWALL—WILLIAM GILPIN—MISTAKES OF OLD GEOGRAPHERS ABOUT THE CAUSES OF THE TEMPERATURE—PECULIAR CLIMATE OF CORNWALL—MR. WERE FOX'S GARDENS — PERPETUAL SPRING — COTTAGE GARDENING SOCIETIES — FLOWERS AND BEES—THE CHOUGH—LOSTWITHIEL—RESTORMEL CASTLE—THE HARVEST AND THE MOWS—FARMS AND FARMERS—INFLUENCE OF ROCKS AND CLIMATE UPON HOUSE BUILDING—THE INNER LIFE OF RICH FAMILIES—HOME OF THE LABOURERS—POLYTECHNIC SOCIETY—FALMOUTH—OPENING OF THE RAILWAY.

An English tourist who had strolled for many years along all the roads in Great Britain and Ireland, once explained to me the motive of his excursions. "I travel," he said to me, "in order to get rid of my selfishness." It would be a rash thing to assert that the same object is aimed at by the innumerable tourists who desert London from the middle of August to the end of September. Most of them leave to instruct themselves and gain a knowledge of their country. And yet does not the man who enlarges the circle of his knowledge also augment the sphere of his sympathies? There is patriotism in their enthusiasm at the sight of the very real beauties which the British isles contain — nests of verdure surrounded by rocks and storms. By communicating with nature, by growing used to the manners of the various counties, and the customs of the different classes that compose a great state, they become less shut up in themselves and participate more widely in the existence of others.

The character of the travelling Englishman undergoes for this very reason a fortunate modification. There are certainly here and there taciturn tourists, inflexible in matters of etiquette, and who never speak to persons to whom they have not been introduced; but they constitute a very rare exception. Most generally the habitual reserve in manner changes into a joyous and cordial expansion, especially with foreigners. The Englishman who has travelled is no longer the same man. I especially refer to the man who has travelled on the Continent; but even those who have traversed the United Kingdom for a lengthened period have shaken off a good deal of prejudice along the road. The influences of a change of locality, and intercourse with fresh scenes and new places, act possibly in even a more striking manner on English women. Immediately after the wedding, the honeymoon is inaugurated, in England, by an excursion lasting some weeks, and intended to consecrate by the festivals of nature the chaste joys of legitimate love. From this day the cost of an autumn trip generally figures in the budget of the household expenses. If, through a concourse of vexatious circumstances, this trip does not take place, and there is an illness in the family during the year, the mother does not fail to attribute it to the want of a change of air. It is possible, too, that the heavy and damp climate of England necessitates a change, and that the English, by renewing their stock of fresh air, are only obeying one of the laws of the national hygiene.

Obeying such a wide-spread custom, I went, towards the end of last summer, into Cornwall. What attracted me to this part of England was a curiosity for novelty and unexpected scenes. Although this county has been intersected for some years by railways, it has preserved—to use a fashionable phrase of the day—a powerful individuality. In spite of its savage rocks and abrupt coasts, it has been less deflowered than other counties by tourists. Besides, a peculiar interest attaches to a county so justly celebrated for the wealth of its mines, and the heroic labours of its miners. Before occupying myself with this great scene of action, I should like to study the general character of the county, and the mode of existence among its inhabitants.

Old Cornwall should be approached by steamer, as by railway the view of the Tamar is to a great extent lost. This river, which has its source in the cold heaths in the north-east of the county, runs a distance of sixty miles, with a thousand coils and bends like a serpent, and falls into Plymouth Straits, displaying at its mouth all the majesty of a great river. The surface of the waves, which are almost as large and agitated as those of the sea, is covered with a fleet at rest. You find there vessels of all shapes and all sizes, from the slim gunboats up to the gigantic three-deckers, which sleep in the shadow of their masts, all ready, as Canning said, to resume their resemblance to living beings, to shake off their wings and arouse their thunder. At a distance these large ships display, flush with the water, a painted mass of large black and white stripes, succeeding each other alternately : the white stripe indicates the row of windows. Among these men-of-war there are some invalided, dismasted, disarmed, ignobly painted a bright yellow, and covered with a roof. These war vessels are now used as sailors' homes.

Leaving on the left, or Cornwall shore, a few curious villages, the steamer arrives at Saltash. Here the eye is attracted by one of the marvels of modern industry; I mean the railway viaduct connecting the counties of Devon and Cornwall. At once strong and light, this bridge, the work of I. K. Brunel, bestrides the turbulent river, leaning in the centre on a single arch with double columns, while other upright and lofty pillars support it on the two banks. The viaduct is nearly half a mile in length. In order to judge the character of this daring construction, you should cross the bridge on foot, between the passage of two trains. Two enormous bent tubes, resembling aerial vaults, bravely support the weight of the chains which suspend in the air the wooden road along which the railway runs. So soon as you have entered this defile, you hear above your head the soughing and voices of the storm; the wind roars, or is entangled, with plaintive notes, in the chains and vibrating iron bars, as in the chords of an immense Æolian harp. At each instant you fancy you can hear behind, in the midst of this prolonged moaning, the thundering sound of a train coming up at full speed. From this elevation (upwards of 150 feet) the river looks like an abyss beneath you. When seen from a distance, the Saltash viaduct bears some resemblance to a triumphal arch. It is the entrance gate that fitted Cornwall, "that sacred land of giants," as it is called in the ambitious language of the old legends.

The Tamar, that moving and winding belt

which separates Devon from Cornwall, is a handsome river. On leaving Saltash and going up as far as Newbridge, it is found to wash singularly picturesque banks or rock walls, covered with a wild vegetation. The traveller who penetrates into Cornwall has necessarily passed through Devon, and he soon notices a great change in the style of the landscape. There is a perfect contrast between the two counties. The soft features of a fertile district are succeeded by a stern country, especially distinguished by the rudeness and grandeur of its lines. There are no tall trees; and the inhabitants of Devon laughingly reproach those of Cornwall with not having sufficient planks of home growth to make a coffin. You see here and there, on the steep slope of the hills, a few woods of young oaks; but these saplings never attain a venerable stature, and are cut down after a certain time to make charcoal. If we wish to understand the nature of this vegetation, which differs in so many essential and striking features from the usual character of an English landscape, we must first form a precise idea of the geographical position and form of Cornwall. The map of England has been compared by humorous geographers to an old woman warming her hands and feet in the setting sun, or, if you prefer it, at the extinct volcanoes of Ireland. These imaginary feet are formed by a promontory that juts out for more than eighty miles into the Atlantic. This promontory is Cornwall, divided through nearly its whole length by a central ridge, with two large watersheds, which grow narrower and become blended toward the point. One of these slopes faces the opening of the Channel, and the other Bristol Straits. This central ridge is composed of a series of hills, more or less high, which commence in Devonshire, and continue, in spite of a few depressions, as far as the Land's End, that is to say, the south-western extremity of England. These hills are mostly lumps of granite rising at regular intervals. They have been compared to enormous vertebræ, which connect the different parts of the county, and at the same time defend this tail of land against the furious attacks of the two seas between which it is situated.

Such a chain of small mountains, embracing an extent of two hundred acres of more or less barren heath, has no speciality to charm the traveller. William Gilpin, an English clergyman at the close of last century, and a descriptive author, advanced in search of the picturesque to the skirt of this barren and desolate region. What was his disenchantment! He suddenly stopped with a broken heart, on the road between Launceston and Bodmin, and turned his back on Cornwall for ever. For my part, through a rather lengthened residence in Kent, I had grown tired of scenery made to please the sight: hence, far from being rebuffed by this sadness of nature, I congratulated myself on finding *en route* what resembled a sombre apparition of the desert in a corner of green England, which is often too much cultivated. These solitudes, with their summits crowned by perpendicular rocks,—these classical heaths and savage ravines, possess a character of desolate grandeur; but, however this may be, Gilpin was greatly mistaken in fancying that all Cornwall was like this. From these arid and frowning heights descend numerous valleys, which extend along the sea-shore, and which, sheltered by the hills against the cutting winds, watered by charming streams or slowly-moving rivulets, and favoured besides by a gentle and moist temperature, are covered nearly all the year with an abundant vegetation. It is in such spots, of course, that we must seek the farms, orchards, and rich crops; but before all, the delicious gardens, which form one of the glories of Cornwall, and which might be called the Paradise of the west of England.

Geographers have now recovered from an old error, which consisted in regarding the celestial system as the sole regulator of climates. A thousand influences, entirely independent of the degrees of distance from the meridian, but more especially the relations between land and sea, exert a sovereign power over the distribution of cold and heat on the surface of our globe. Entirely local causes, they create very frequently a peculiar effect in the general climate of a country. How far is this the case with certain parts of Cornwall? Before answering such a question, we must consult the flowers, those organic thermometers, whose testimony cannot be false. In various parts of the county, but always near the sea-shore, we are astonished at finding in the front gardens of the houses ornamental plants, which remain out of doors all the year, and do not belong at all to the general flora of England. Myrtles, laurels, fuchsias, pomegranates, and hortensias attain a remarkable size, flourish bravely in the open air, and form hedges, clumps, and fragrant screens which elegantly adorn the windows and walls.

Many other surprises awaited me at Grove Hill, the charming residence of Mr. Robert Were Fox, a well-known savant and member of the Royal Society. His house contains magnificent pictures, rare china, and a rich collection of animals; but I was more struck by the beauty of his gardens, which have justly been compared with those of the Hesperides. The orange, date, and lemon-trees pass the winter here in the open air, grow freely, and bear ripe fruit. I saw a tree there from which 123 lemons were plucked in one day, all excellent, and much sweeter than those sold at the shops. You might believe yourself in Italy or Spain, but it is a damp Spain, for the grass grows abundantly, and the foliage of the trees offers the eye the same vigorous tint of deep blue-green which distinguishes the vegetation in the other English counties. Mr. Fox has naturalized more than 300 exotic species; he has thus brought together the plants of Australia and New Zealand, the trees of cold countries and those of hot countries, loaded all the year round with flowers and fruit; large aloes, not imprisoned in a box or under glass houses, but planted freely in the ground, form arcades which might be called natural. The most extraordinary thing is, that these trees have not, at Grove Hill, the stunted look which is generally noticed in the productions of hot countries which have changed their climate: on the contrary, they grow as if they were at home.

In addition to Grove Hill, which stands on one of the last hills of Falmouth, Mr. Were Fox possesses, in the neighbourhood, a country house at Pengerrick, whose situation is really admirable, and where I spent several days amid all the delicate attentions of English hospitality. In front of the house stretches out a vast lawn, terminating in a clump of tall trees, cut through about the centre to offer a prospect of the distant sea. Forests of rhododendrons and camellias grow with wild profusion in the beds, from which also rise the unctuous and thorny plants of the torrid zones. Cornwall is well situated at the southwest of England, where it forms a sort of peninsula; but this single circumstance, though evidently favourable, would not at all suffice to explain why certain parts of that county enjoy a special climate, forming such a marked contrast with the general climate of Great Britain. What, then, is the principal cause of these phenomena of temperature, which I was also enabled to remark at Carclew, in the magnificent gardens of Sir Charles Lemon? This side of Cornwall is warmed during winter by a submarine current that reaches it from the Gulf of Mexico, or the Gulf Stream.

The southern character of Cornwall, however, must not be exaggerated through faith in the flowers. Tropical plants grow there in a sort which, after all, has nothing tropical about it. The whole secret of this acclimatized vegetation consists in the absence of winter, or, at least, in a winter stripped of all its rigours. During this season, the sea is four or five degrees warmer than the land, and the little snow that falls at times melts immediately on the coast. Christmas, so celebrated in other English counties through its wreath of hoar-frost, arrives, on the contrary, along the hollow, sheltered roads of the western coasts amid a perfect festival of nature, from which even foliage is not absent. This part of Cornwall is consequently, as may be supposed, the one where the first signs of vegetation are found in spring, and where the flowers spring at one bound from their winter sleep. According to observations which I collected at Polperro, Falmouth, and Penzance, the seasons are some weeks more advanced there than in the north of Italy: they generally agree with Naples. This advantage lasts till the end of March: in April the conditions are nearly equal; but in the following months Cornwall loses what it had gained, and the superiority turns decidedly in favour of the hot countries. It results from this comparative scale of climates that the south-west coast of Cornwall is one of the spots where there is the least difference between winter and summer. The sea, in short, exerts over it that power of equalizing the seasons which is frequently one of the characteristics of its relations with the land.

Such a relative uniformity naturally suggests the idea of a perpetual spring, and such it is nearly all the year in Cornwall; but I am bound to add that it is generally a rainy spring. How do the plants of New Zealand, Australia, and Florida grow accustomed to the conditions of such a climate? We must believe that even tropical trees have less need of heat than they fear the cold. Would it be the same with animals foreign to our northern regions? I regret, in the interests of natural history, that the experiment has not been tried, and that the savants of Cornwall, after conquering the vegetation of the south, have not extended the same care to the acclimatization of certain living creatures.

Cultivation, which is everywhere modelled on the laws of temperature and climate, evidently was bound to take advantage of the mild winter and premature springs of Cornwall. It has devoted itself especially to what in France is called *primeurs*. From Christmas up to the beginning of May it sends by rail to Covent Garden market precocious vegetables, which naturally fetch a good price. London has, in this way, its winter kitchen-garden on the west coast. By the side of sumptuous gardens devoted to science and pleasure, you find in Cornwall other gardens which have an eye to the useful. In nearly all the towns there is a cottage-gardening society, which, as its name indicates, is formed to encourage cottage-gardening. There is an annual exhibition, at which a jury solemnly award prizes for the finest fruit, flowers, and vegetables. I have attended several of these interesting shows, which have quite the character of rural fêtes. The exhibitor must have cultivated his produce himself; and I saw at Tavistock a magnificent bouquet, whose sole fault was that it was fraudulent. After that, trust to the innocence of flowers! A placard announced that the exhibitor's name had been erased from the list of prizes, for claiming the labour and merit of another man. I also admired baskets of fruit which would have done honour to the most fortunate climates; if they had a defect in my eyes, it was that they were too fine, for they might easily have been taken for artificial fruit. These institutions, in which women take a special interest in some parts, certainly render great services. Horticultural emulation thus adds greatly to the comforts and ornaments of domestic life in the homes of the working classes. Some of these societies do not restrict themselves to spreading the advantages and taste for gardening through all classes, but also employ their influence in obtaining for working men plots of ground, which is often very difficult in the interior, or even in the neighbourhood of towns.

Cornwall is the county of flowers, and hence we must not be surprised at finding bees amid all these flowers. Most of the hives are clumsily made of a truss of straw fastened at the top; but it may be supposed that the insect cares little about the external beauty of its domicile, for it attaches itself faithfully to it. I saw several of these hives in the garden of a Quaker gentleman. This venerable sect professes a species of universal benevolence, which extends to all the animals of creation: hence the owner of these bees carefully refrained from robbing them of the fruit of their labour. It is his principle that the maker of the honey ought to eat it too. Many other inhabitants of Cornwall do not display such scruples; and I have known humble cottagers derive a considerable profit from the toil of these industrious insects.

The mildness of the winter also attracts to this county a number of birds, which either heighten the pleasures of the latter or the charms of country life. Among the latter, there is a curious one, quite peculiar to Cornwall, which the inhabitants call chough. It is a black bird, very certainly belonging to the crow family, with the singularity that it has a red bill and claws. In a wild state, it inhabits solitary and inaccessible rocks; but it has the misfortune of being in great request with ornithologists; the country lads wage an obstinate war with it, and scramble in spring to the brink of the most frightful precipices in order to rob its nest. The chough, in spite of its suspicious character and the stern nature of the spots it haunts when in a state of liberty, is very easily tamed. I saw one at a country house, and it appeared completely reconciled with its new home. This bird is becoming very scarce, and there are reasons for fearing that it will entirely disappear in the course of time. A poor family, who had succeeded in capturing a young couple of choughs, sent them recently to the Prince of Wales, who requited the service by a present of a five-pound note. It must not be forgotten that the Prince of Wales is at the same time Duke of Cornwall.

I visited at Lostwithiel, the offices of the Duchy.* The name of this town is a contraction of " lost within the hills ;" and the name is well suited to it, for it is situated on the banks of the Fowey, in a hollow, quite commanded by verdant hills. You reach it by crossing an old, curiously-built bridge, surmounted by a zig-zag parapet. The offices of the Duchy of Cornwall are in an old castle, a part of which was for a time converted into a prison, and which still offers, even in old age, a rather noble appearance, with its lofty windows and Gothic gates. I saw there large maps designed with minute care, and indicating by various colours what parts of the county belong to the Duchy and which not. The share of the Duchy is certainly very considerable. The origin of this Duchy, and the way in which it came into the possession of the Prince of Wales, are as follows :—According to the old English law, all the mines belong to the Crown, because they supply the necessary materials for coining money, a privilege which belongs to the sovereign exclusively. Hence it comes that the moors of Dartmoor and Cornwall, so rich in metal, were regarded ages

* The chief office is in London. At the head of the Mining department is Mr. Warington Smyth, Professor at the Museum of Practical Geology. It was owing to the kindness of this gentleman that I was enabled to study certain details in Cornwall, quite inaccessible to strangers.

ago as royal property, when, in the year 1333, Edward III. made them a gift to his eldest son, the Black Prince, and to his heirs, the eldest sons of the kings and queens of England, in perpetuity. This was formed by charter the Duchy of Cornwall, which was not only composed of land, more or less metalliferous, but also of castles, parks, manors, towns, villages, and a forest full of deer.

Among the estates attached to it at the present day, I will merely mention a charming walk which leads from Lostwithiel to the ruins of Restormel Castle. This edifice was formerly used as a residence by the earls of Cornwall. Nothing is left now but the circular walls, which are nine feet in thickness, and built like a crown on the point of a grassy hill. These ruins, covered with masses of ivy, certainly form what the English call a romantic scene. People go there from the environs for picnics and parties of pleasure. I have seen ivy, in different parts of Great Britain, cultivated along garden walls, or growing spontaneously among ruins, with the advantage a damp climate offers it; but I never saw any so vigorous as at Restormel Castle. It reveals a sort of touching friendship for the remains of this old castle, which it clasps in its sturdy arms, and part of which it supports in the air. Ivy is one of the favourite plants of the Englishman. He sees in it a symbol of those strong and tenacious affections, but more especially of those pious family sentiments which connect the memories of the past, like dissevered stones.

At the time when I visited Cornwall—from the middle of August to the middle of September—the harvest could be seen in all its varied stages of development. As I went along, I saw ripe wheat still standing; corn laid on the ground by the hook; corn made into sheaves and arranged at regular distances. A custom exists here which is not at all met with in other counties. After the field has been reaped, a handful of ears is left standing, which is called the neck. Cutting the neck of the harvest is a ceremony performed with simple solemnity. The reapers are drawn up in a circle, and before one of them lays a hook upon this last sheaf, they sing, or rather say, "I have one, I have one, I have one!" "What have you? what have you? what have you?" "A neck, a neck, a neck." The chorus raises three vigorous hurrahs; and the neck, decorated with flowers and ribbons, is carried to the farm, where the day is usually terminated by some draughts of ale, or even by a rustic banquet; during which a currant cake smokes in the centre of the table. This peculiarity, which dates back to immemorial time, is not the only one that distinguishes a Cornish harvest.

Instead of immediately constructing the stacks, as is the custom in all other English counties, temporary heaps of sheaves are formed in the field, which are called assish, or wind-mows. These heaps are of a conical shape, are about twelve feet high, and contain from two to three hundred sheaves, which are all turned inwards. One or several men thus arrange them on the harvest day, by the help of a wooden fork; and these cones are then covered with a roof of straw or reeds. The mows, which are arranged twenty or thirty together, remind you of a Huron village, when seen at a distance. This perfectly local custom is evidently founded on the uncertainty of the climate: the wheat piled in this manner is perfectly sheltered from the rain, while the straw, which is generally greasy and damp when cut, has time to dry under the influence of the wind and sun. They are left thus in the field for some weeks; at the expiration of which the farmer, choosing his day and hour, proceeds to carry them and form a stack. The latter is generally made near the house, and is built upon a platform supported by very short round-headed pillars—enormous granite mushrooms—and forms a considerable mass, of very substantial and regular architecture. In some parts of Cornwall, for instance round St. Just, the wheat-fields offer another remarkable singularity. In the centre is a basket of cabbage, whose coarse green and large leaves form a strange contrast with the golden hue of the ripe corn. Under this mound the labourers bury the stubble of the last harvest, and all sorts of vegetable detritus which by decomposition forms a decent manure.

The English, in their agriculture, always think of two sorts of produce, bread and meat. They naturally look to the fields for the means of breeding horned cattle. In spite of a surface covered to a large extent by rocks and heather, Cornwall possesses fertile valleys, wonderfully sheltered and watered by small streams, which possess a strange character. As they are nearly all subject to the ebb and flow of the sea, they assume a perfectly different aspect according to the hour when you see them. There are moments when they seem to have utterly disappeared; of the fresh current of water which you noticed in the morning, nothing remains but a damp and muddy bed. I have seen horses cross these dried-up streams and graze on the blades of grass which grow, it might be said, between two tides. In the fields bordering these capricious watercourses, you see the Durham short-horns, the handsome Devon breeds, with their graceful and symmetrical shapes; but before all the small Cornish breed, which, being after all best adapted to the conditions of the climate and the nature of the climate, supplies an abundant and renowned milk. It is of this milk that the farmers make the celebrated clotted cream, of which, it is said, rightly or wrongly, the Prince of Wales retains a sweet reminiscence among the other reminiscences of childhood. By the side of these horned cattle graze peaceably the Welsh pony, which is used to draw the heavy carts, and the small grey horse, a native of Cornwall, which, when crossed with thoroughbreds, performs lighter tasks; but what surprised me most was to find in this enclosure of verdure red sheep, the sight of which reminded me of Candide's sheep in Eldorado. I at first thought that this colour came from the ferruginous tinge of the earth on which they live; but I learnt afterwards that it was the result of an artificial process intended to preserve them against the insects which get into wool.

The farms are generally of small size, especially if compared with those in other English counties. A part of the land is in the hands of a respectable class of farmers, who have taken it for three lives, and whose lease is ordinarily renewed in perpetuity. This system, however, is falling off to a great extent, and most of the farms are now let on a seven or fourteen years' lease. The buildings, formed of large stones, whose contexture varies according to the geological character of the district, are distinguished in every case by a look of great substantiality. In them resides a family generally numerous, in which are displayed all the ages of humanity, from the grandfather to the newly-born child in its mother's arms. Their mode of living is extremely simple; the labourers and hinds dine at the same table with the farmer's family. This table is very frugal: salt meat or fish, dumplings and boiled potatoes, form the staple food. The farmers, as well as the labourers, only drink water or tea, except, perhaps, at harvest time, when they allow themselves a little beer. By the side of this, it is surprising to find in each interior a great air of comfort and delicate cleanliness.

The sons are often well educated; the girls, active and coquettish, do the honours of the house to strangers with a modesty that has nothing awkward about it. It may be said, in a certain sense, that there are no peasants left. London fashions are found in the most humble farms. We have often laughed at the pictures in which the shepherdesses of the last century guard their flocks in hooped dresses. Well, I saw cows milked in Cornwall by girls with the same artificial outline — the fashionable steel hoops had been merely substituted for the old baskets under their wide skirts. All this dressing does not prevent them from working bravely. In some of these farms as many as thirty or forty oxen are fattened at once. At the same time, the stables, poultry-yard, and dairy must be looked after. It is true that machinery does a large part of the work, and assists the industrious arms:—there are such to winnow the corn, cut the chaff, clean the barley and oats, and prepare the food of the cattle. The motive power which imparts life to these machines is most frequently a water-wheel, situated near the farm-buildings.

In all countries two circumstances have had a notable influence on the architecture of the house —the geological character and the climate. As for the former, Cornwall rests on old Silurian and Devonian rocks, which rend the surface of the soil at various spots, and present almost inexhaustible stone quarries. Coarse limestone, which is only found at Plymouth and its vicinity; porphyry, which is principally used for works of art; schistous or slate rocks, what is here called greenstone; the elvans—excellent building stone—have in turn supplied ample and solid materials for human habitations. The houses, built of different-coloured stones, form interesting groups in the towns and villages. Some of these houses are built with taste, while others, on the contrary, are made of shreds and patches. The latter, after all, are not the least curious. In them human industry has been satisfied with collecting irregular stones, and cementing them together with a sort of mortar made of porcelain earth. These white lines run between the dark masses, and they form, as it were, the letters of a mysterious alphabet on the rough frontage of the cottages.

As you advance towards the Land's End, you meet with granite. This royal stone, in some parts, only costs the trouble of picking it up. Hence we may expect to see the most humble cottages, and even pigstyes, built of the massive fragments of the Cyclopean rock. Brick houses, in London a necessity of the soil, only figure here as the whim of rich men, who wish to distinguish themselves from the crowd. Granite, in fact, has the fault, in Cornwall, of being too common; instead of being proud of the beauty of this rock, whose close grain and spangles of mica sparkle in the sun, it is but too often hidden by an ignoble coat of whitewash. One of the qualities of the stone is to impart to houses a character for solidity. At St. Just, and in other towns, the huge chimneys look on the roofs like bastions, and this was necessary to resist the blasts from the sea. These houses last for ages; and it is no uncommon thing to find in them old men who remember that their father and grandfather saw the light and died beneath the same hospitable roof. Does not granite, too, exert an influence over the manner of building and the style of architecture? Being of itself a stern, hard stone, rebellious to the chisel, it naturally engendered in the fine arts a character of grandeur and simplicity: such are, in fact, the features noticeable in Penzance in the architecture of the wealthy houses.

The climate has also been consulted by the builders. Naturalists have recently discovered that the integument of animals was to a great extent determined by the conditions of the external medium in which they live. Can it be the same, up to a certain point, with the external covering of houses? Before entering Cornwall, the traveller is greatly surprised at finding, in Wiltshire and Devon, old houses covered with tiles, not merely on the roof, which would not be at all extraordinary, but also on the front facing the street. Such a casing gives these houses the look of immense reptiles, and, I must add, owing to the tranquillity prevailing in these old buildings, sleeping reptiles. This is evidently an armour against the furious rains of spring and autumn.

In Cornwall, the same system has often been adopted for a similar cause; the only difference is in the character of the materials supplied by the ground. In the latter county slate rocks abound; hence we may expect to find a screen of slates substituted for the cuirass of tiles. For a reason equally founded on the nature of the country, the massive granite cottages at the Land's End have low, narrow windows, like the loopholes in a fortress. Who does not see in this a precaution of the inhabitants against the seawinds? Modern builders, it is true, have neglected these various indications of the climate in the construction of wealthy houses; but they trust to science and more expensive resources to hold at bay the severity of the seasons.

We will now enter some of these houses, and

learn the mode of life in them. I will selec first the type of an English gentleman's family. One of the great advantages of Cornwall is, that the landed gentry like to live on their estates, and watch themselves the agricultural improvements. In France, rich persons pass a few summer months at their chateau, and then return to Paris to seek government offices or indulge in winter amusements. In England, where there are few places to give away, and where London is not a capital of pleasures, things happen very differently. What are called provincial manners among us are nowhere found in the United Kingdom. In the counties you find women as distinguished and minds as well cultivated as in the capital. There are classes, I allow, but there are no distances. The gentleman is the same from one end of Great Britain to the other.

The anxiety of the latter, when in the country, is to create himself a moral independence: instead of going to London, he attracts London to his house. To do this, he receives new books, the reviews, and papers; he is glad to have at his table travellers whom he knows, or who are recommended to him. The arrangement of his house offers a character of neatness and simplicity in wealth. At eight or nine in the morning the whole household is up. The family meet in the breakfast-room, when the daughters give the mother and father the morning kiss — in the

English fashion, on one cheek—and where the stranger receives the serious and affectionate salutations of the family. A door opens, and all the servants, frequently seven or eight in number, enter one after the other, and in silence. When all are assembled, prayers are read, or else, in some sects, a chapter of the Bible is read. These religious customs may astonish a stranger; but in England, where the difference of ranks is so marked, there is something touching in this admission of the servants to the bosom of the family, that all may perform in common what is regarded as a duty toward the Deity. When prayers are over, the family collect round the table, and drink tea or coffee. After breakfast, while the master is generally engaged with his studies or business, the visitor has to occupy his hours agreeably—a large library, scientific collections, green-houses embellished with rare plants, and the gardens surrounding the house. At one o'clock there is lunch, or what we call in France the second breakfast. In the afternoon, the family drive out to pay visits, explore the neighbourhood, or keep up with the farms and cottages those kindly relations which, to a certain point, fill up the difference of condition and persons in English society. At six o'clock comes dinner: the ladies have changed their dress, and the gentlemen are in evening costume. The conversation, less animated and sparkling than in

France, generally turns on serious subjects. One of the peculiarities of an English dinner is, that after dessert the ladies rise and leave the dining-room, while the gentlemen seat themselves again, and drink a few glasses of port and sherry. There is no hob-nobbing; but the master of the house who wishes to do honour to his guest, invites him to fill his glass; he does the same himself, and the couple exchange a bow before drinking. About half-an-hour later all the company are assembled in the drawing-room, which the servants enter in procession at about eleven o'clock. Evening prayers are then read, after which everybody retires to his bed-room, after a friendly shake of the hand from all the members of the family. I am greatly afraid this mode of life will appear very solemn and regular, if measured by the standard of French manners; and yet in these homes you seem to inhale a perfume of domesticity and hospitality.

It will be, perhaps, curious to contrast such houses, in which an honourable opulence prevails, with the life in the cottages of the labourers: this is the general name given here to tillers of the soil. A single ground-floor room serves at once as kitchen, dining and drawing-room. A wide open chimney, without a grate—a rare circumstance across the Channel—proves that it was not originally intended to burn coals. The combustible formerly in use was roots, prickly furze, and dried turf, which, when raised in slabs, forms a species of peat. At the present day this is more or less mingled with coal. A wooden or stone bench, placed in the interior of the chimney, serves as the family seat during the cold winter evenings. The labourers frequently obtain from the farmer their supply of gorse and dry grass, on condition of returning him the ashes. A deal table, without a cloth, but carefully scrubbed, receives the coarse and substantial dishes which have been cooked in front of the fire on a hot plate of iron. The whole family sit round this table on massive benches, generally fastened to the wall. If there be by chance an old chair in the house, it is reserved for the grandmother. The children are more or less well tended, according to the character of the place or the persons. I saw in some poor cottages little girls, barefooted and with their hair floating in disorder down their backs, who reminded one of Ireland; and yet the stranger is struck by the beauty of these brats, even when dressed in rags. Their large black eyes; their complexion, rather brightened than burnt by the sun; and their robust and well-proportioned limbs, evidently denote a great race.

Though the toilette of these persons may be more or less neglected, the room is generally very clean: the floor, washed every morning, is often sprinkled with fine sand, through which the whiteness of the boards is visible. The wives, and the daughters as soon as they have acquired the necessary strength, attend out of doors in the stalls and fields, to all sorts of rustic tasks; hence it is not unusual to find during day-time these cottages only guarded by a housekeeper of twelve years of age. And that is not all, for the door remains open from morn till night to all comers, with the simple confidence of persons who have nothing to defend. The labourers regularly employed by a farmer also generally obtain their wheat at a moderate price, fixed beforehand for the whole year; those, on the other hand, who are not in regular employment, arrange with the farmer for a piece of land, which they cultivate. In this case they naturally pay rent, or surrender a part of the crop. With the remainder of the crop, which most usually consists of potatoes, the labourer manages to feed a pig, pay the rent of his cottage, and even rear some poultry. The family, more or less dispersed during the week, only comes together on the Saturday night and Sunday. I sought in vain, even at those times, for the scenes of domestic joy and happiness so sweetly described by English poets. The peasants, as a rule, speak little; and it is rather difficult to discover the reason for this silence, which at times resembles coldness. Is it indifference for their mode of life? Is it resignation, or that species of tacit contentment which the consciousness of a strict duty accomplished imparts to a man?

In the towns, several learned societies have, during later years, greatly aided to develop agriculture as well as to increase the knowledge and improve the morals of the population. London is not at all like Paris, an absorbing centre which attracts all great intellects; and, in despite of Voltaire's saying, provincial academies are in several parts of England—wise daughters that make themselves talked about. Among these institutions, I will merely mention the Polytechnic Society, founded in 1833. Although it owes its origin to two sisters, the Misses Fox, there is nothing feminine about it; it holds annual meetings at Falmouth, at which questions of science, political economy, and industry, are discussed. Latterly several discoveries and useful improvements have been made by its members.

The charming town of Falmouth was well selected to serve as the place for these learned meetings, for these lectures, and these annual exhibitions, which attract a great number of curious persons from the surrounding country. Situated at the mouth of the river Fal, which forms at this spot a magnificent estuary, and on the undulating shores of a narrow and deep bay, it naturally enjoys an excellent port, commanded by pretty hills, between which run verdant valleys. Nature has done much for Falmouth, and its inhabitants have done more than nature. They love their town—such was the remark of one of them—as a woman is loved. Hence they have not recoiled from any sacrifice to add to the beauty of the site useful works which might attract vessels to a port already convenient and spacious. The number of these vessels, which was only 1519 in 1850, had risen in 1860 to 2800. The docks, which are not yet finished, are, however, a most imposing building. Two breakwaters, supported by a double row of scaffolding filled with massive stones, advance into the sea for a distance of 1028 feet, and protect the interior of the port by breaking the impetuosity of the waves. Two graving docks, vast granite basins, are of use to repair ships; while spacious quays run for a length of 640 feet, and protect by their stone breastplates land recently conquered from the sea. How could a population of 5000 or 6000 inhabitants find the resources necessary for the completion of these great works, without counting those which are now in progress? This is an enigma, the explanation of which must be asked of that spirit of self-confidence, a fruit of the centralization and liberty which forms the strength of the provinces in England.

At the moment when I arrived at Falmouth, the entire population was on the eve of a festival. The opening of a railway, which in a few days would connect the town with Truro, as the great artery of Cornwall, was about to take place. The long narrow street, which runs through the whole town with an undulating curve, with a few side streets on the left, through which a glimpse of the port can be obtained, was already decorated at regular distances with arches of foliage. Sailors of all nations, and talking all languages, from Russian to Greek and Armenian, were walking about in bands amid these joyous preparations. The first train that reached Falmouth station was greeted by the energetic hurrahs of the sailors, volunteers, foresters, odd-fellows, and all the good citizens of the town. A banquet, to which I had the honour of being invited, brought together the principal inhabitants of Falmouth, and several M.P.s, in a large shed decorated with garlands. The toasts, which were produced with a thorough English warmth, I fear, would have slightly tickled the humour of the author of *Pickwick*; but this local ambition which wishes to do everything for itself, and promises itself the empire of the world, has after all something respectable at bottom.

On the very day of opening the line, a dead whale arrived in the port, towed by Falmouth sailors. It had caught itself among the Cagenith rocks, and had killed itself by struggling. This event was interpreted by several persons as a presage of the future greatness of

Falmouth, and as a homage paid by the monster to this maritime city: *ipse capi voluit*. It is certain, however, that the recently-opened railway will make a new town of Falmouth, and all it wants now is to get back the service of the transatlantic mail-boats.

The commerce of the town has greatly increased, the navigation has extended along the coasts, and agriculture has made considerable progress inland, but all this only represents the smallest part of the wealth of Cornwall. Its most productive fields and most abundant crops rest in the bowels of the earth, and sometimes even under the bed of the ocean.

CHAPTER II.

A SILVER MINE—THE ENGLISH MONT ST. MICHEL—THE PHŒNICIANS IN CORNWALL—THE JEWS AND MARAZION—EXTERIOR OF THE COPPER AND TIN MINES—CARCLAZE—CHINA CLAY—SAINT AUSTEL—SUBMARINE MINES—BOTALLACK—WHERRY MINE—CAMBORNE AND REDRUTH—CARN-BREA—MINING SPECULATIONS—THE ADVENTURERS—THE GREAT ADIT—LOOE POOL, OR THE RED LAKE—LENGTH OF THE LADDERS—MAN-ENGINE—ACCIDENTS PECULIAR TO MINERS—PAY DAY—SALES BY AUCTION—EDUCATION OF THE MINERS—THEIR MANNERS—COQUETRY OF THE WOMEN—THE PACK-MAN—SUNDAY IN CORNWALL—PHILOSOPHY OF DRESS.

CORNWALL is the county of metals: lead, iron, cobalt, bismuth, and uranium are found there in larger or smaller quantities. Near Lostwithiel, I visited, on a hill whence the eye surveys an horizon of verdure and a panorama of valleys, a mine of silver mixed with copper and antimony. After the failure of the first company, this mine was reopened, four years ago, by a fresh one. A steam-engine to pump out the water had been attached to the underground works. It has occurred more than once that worthless mines have been made to pay by the intervention of the superior forces which industry now has at its disposition. This mine now produces twenty tons of ore per month, and the value of each ton is estimated at £10. Silver is also extracted, and even in large quantities, from the lead mines. I saw at Mr. Fox's a silver tea-urn made out of a Cornish ingot. But the characteristic features of the mineralogy of the county is the presence of copper, and, before all, of tin.

The abundance of the two last metals has favoured in Cornwall, since time immemorial, the development of the mining trade. Diodorus Siculus states that the ancient Britons loaded tin on wicker boats covered with leather, and carried it thus to the island of Ictis. Where is this Ictis? Persons have fancied they have found it in St. Michael's Mount, an island at high water and a peninsula when the sea retires.* Timœus, the historian, who lived in the time of Pliny, tells us also that the same Britons tore tin out of the rocks, and carried it in chariots to the neighbouring islands at low water. One of these, in addition to St. Michael's Mount, was, doubtless, Looe Island, situated near the coast, a few miles from Liskeard. From these various points of embarkation the tin was loaded in Phœnician ships, which conveyed it to Tyre and Sidon. It is

* In history, the St. Michael's Mount of Cornwall has been frequently confounded with Mont Saint Michel, near St. Malo. Both are alternately separated from the coast, and rejoined to it by the tidal movement, and both have been a monastery; but the English Mont St. Michel, more fortunate than ours, has never been a prison.

supposed that the bronzes of Assyria and Egypt were made of this metal, which was employed at a very early age in the arts. The tin trade even attracted Jews to the west coast of England long prior to the Norman conquest, perhaps even before the fall of Jerusalem. There are in Cornwall many old localities bearing their name, such as Bojewyan (in Celtic, the abode of the Jews), Trejewas (the village of the Jews), and Marazion, or Bitter Zion (*mara* or *amara* Zion). What, in truth, can be more bitter than the memory of an absent or down-trodden country? This last village was formerly a great metal market in the hands of the Jews.

I saw in a collection of minerals and antiquities some curious specimens of blocks of tin, such as were prepared for trade in the infancy of the mines. Among these specimens is a mass of stone covered, or rather purposely concealed, by a thin layer of metal, thus proving that fraud is ancient in the world. At various spots are found traces of diggings made either by the Britons themselves or by their successors, the Romans and Saxons, but which in any case date back to a remote antiquity. These excavations, made almost on the surface of the soil, are very curious and picturesque; they form, after centuries, caverns more or less obscure, frequently obstructed at their entrance by brambles, sometimes decorated inside with stalactites, and lined with graceful moss growing between the rocks. Some of these galleries are rather extensive, but of no depth at all; at that day the art of digging air shafts and getting rid of the subterranean waters was unknown.

The tin or copper mines may be recognized at some distance off by a narrow house surmounted by a pointed roof, which bears considerable resemblance to a windmill. In front of this house rise to a considerable height two large beams, which separate at the base, are connected toward the point by a cross-bar, and thus form a truncated angle. The top of this wooden construction is at times bare, at others surmounted by a dry branch, a flag, or a weathercock. At night, on the desolate and wild moors, they look like instruments of punishment, enormous gibbets put up in front of the hills to menace the traveller. Around this scaffolding are piles of earth, heaps of stone and clay, and rocks broken by the hammer. These are the very entrails of the mine. This rubbish indicates on the surface the extent and direction of the subterranean works, as well as the nature of the sub-soil. The progress of the mines in the ground has been justly compared to that of the mole throwing out the materials which it displaces in opening a passage for itself. Clumsy wooden aqueducts, supported by rude pillars, sometimes convey to an extraordinary distance the water that issues from the interior of the mine. Seen from a distance, these mines seem deserted; silent, but every now and then a jet of steam bursts from them. As you go along, you notice works in every imaginable stage of development or decadence: there are mines in embryo— mines which, as they say here, have reached the age of manhood—tottering mines and dead mines. The last, with their empty houses fallen into ruins, their abandoned shafts, whence a deathlike smell issues, and their works invaded by the grass, awake a feeling of deep melancholy.

If we approach a working mine, a sort of fortress surrounded by ramparts of rubbish, we find ourselves among machinery that amazes us by its grandeur, and which spontaneously performs a series of mysterious movements. Some wave in the air their wooden arms with the gestures of our old telegraphs, while others, made of iron, advance and draw back on the surface of the ground. All these manœuvres, which are difficult of comprehension, may give rise to the most fantastic ideas; we might imagine ourselves transported to another planet, among beings certainly endowed with the faculty of acting, but whose life we cannot at all understand. Certain sounds soon bring the visitor back to the reality. At times songs burst forth from the buildings, and the voices of girls and children may be recognized. Here and there is seen a wearied man, whose canvas clothes are quite damp and stained by a reddish mud; it is a miner who has just ascended the shaft. The situation of the mines also adds greatly to the character of the works. Some of them stand in the midst of a pleasant landscape, whose surface they rend; but generally the chief groups are situated on immense moors, rendered gloomy by a sullen sky and bounded by barren hills. As soon as you approach the great metallic centres, vegetation disappears, either because man, occupied with gathering the wealth of the sub-soil, has neglected agriculture, or because the earth refuses to prove doubly fertile. Several of the copper and tin mines, indeed, are situated amid the wildest scenes of nature.

One of the most curious is that of Carclaze, three miles from Saint Austel, a small town with a fine old church. A road runs to a large common, all covered with furze and gorse. As the bushes were studded with golden flowers, I did not complain of the sterility of the soil; and besides, the sea could be seen in all its grandeur at a certain distance. All at once an abyss opens in the gloomy common, before which you halt in stupefaction. The origin of this prodigious excavation, which is at least a mile in circumference and more than 150 feet in depth, has been attributed by the ignorant to the intervention of Satan, by the learned to the Romans or the Anglo-Saxons. It is not a mine properly so called, but a quarry, an open air-shaft; the workmen are streamers, that is to say, men who obtain tin by washing the deposits found by the disaggregation of the primitive rocks. The interior of this abyss, whose greyish whiteness contrasts with the colour of the common and the brown surface of the moors that surround it, displays masses of granite; but it is a softened granite, decomposed by certain influences which are not yet thoroughly known. Along the flanks of the precipice run at various stages narrow paths by which the workmen ascend and descend, while others dig into the rocks in order to find the metal in them. At regular distances, too, there are in these depths wheels, tramways, and wooden conduits full of water. These wheels set in motion hammers that crush the ore; the running water carries off this pulverized matter into reservoirs, in which the tin separates from the granite. The metal thus purified forms under water strata which are afterwards dug out. Very considerable quantities of tin have been extracted during centuries by this very simple process. The workmen, however, complain that the mine will not yield as much as it formerly did, hence several of them have turned their attention to another product.

In the same excavation, but on the other side of the quarry, and facing the tin works, a torrent, at first yellow, but which soon changes its colour, and becomes of a milky white, falls over projecting rocks. Men armed with picks feed this torrent by casting into it lumps of white earth. After running thus to the bottom of the abyss, which it crosses at one bound, the stream suddenly disappears under an arch. You might suppose it lost, but it can be easily found again; to do so, it is only necessary to go five or six hundred yards along the common and find a fresh scene of operations. Here the white stream reappears, and is received in reservoirs or cisterns. The milky fluid, by remaining still, deposits at the bottom of these cisterns a sort of cream, above which the water is perfectly limpid and blue. The action of the wind and sun is sufficient to evaporate the water in a few months. The white clay is then cut out with a knife or a spade, and is carried to open sheds to dry: it here hardens and forms the matter used in making china.

Up to the middle of the last century, the art of making china was almost unknown in England. A white earth, kaolin, which had long been supposed peculiar to China, was wanting for the purpose. In 1745, an adventurer brought back from Virginia this same substance, which, owing to its rarity, sold at that time for thirteen guineas a ton. Ten years later, William Cockworthy, a Plymouth Quaker, formed a partnership with Lord Camelford, to work on an estate belonging to the latter at St. Stephen, a vein of white clay, since known by the name of Cornish kaolin. The experiment having succeeded, he established at Plymouth a china manufactory, which was afterwards transferred to Bristol. Cockworthy thus laid the foundation of a trade which was speedily developed. At the present day these clay works are widely spread over certain parts of Cornwall, especially in the neighbourhood of Saint Austel. The primary matter of the factories presents itself in a state of nature under two very distinct shapes: china clay and china stone. We have seen how the first is collected, and the details of the process merely vary according to the spot and the nature of the water.

Some of these works are very interesting, and employ a very large number of persons, men, women, and children. The women have white bonnets, white sleeves, and white aprons, and it is curious to see them carrying to the surrounding hills a clay whiter still, which they artistically expose to the sunbeams. The china stone, on the contrary, is obtained by the process most generally employed in quarries, that is to say, blasting the rock. When it has been cut out, it is placed in carts and conveyed to the nearest port, whence it is at once carried in ships to the Staffordshire and Worcestershire factories. More than 80,000 tons are thus annually exported from Cornwall, representing a value of £240,000, and about 7000 persons are employed, either in extracting or transporting this article. Whether found in the shape of clay or stone, Cornish kaolin is certainly produced by the decomposition of the granite, or at least of the felspath which enters into the texture of the granite. At Carclaze the various stages of this decomposition may be observed in the rocks, along which the workmen collect either tin or china clay.

Mines, properly so called, differ from the stream works of Carclaze, in that, instead of seeking the metal in an open excavation, the workmen pursue it, on the contrary, under ground in dark galleries. The most picturesque are, undeniably, the famous submarine mines on the north-west coast of Cornwall, in the vicinity of Saint Just. Among the latter, which have all a grand character, must first be mentioned the United Mines. These run quite close to the cape of Cornwall; a vast pile of rocks, which advance proudly into the sea. A group of houses, intended to protect the steam-engines, is perched on the point of lofty cliffs rent by gunpowder or attacked by the pick. These rocks, which defied time, have been crushed by man. These red mines form a contrast with the black surface of the other rocks which border it. The mine opposes to the sea on this side a sort of platform resembling the prow of a vessel. The works run along fearful precipices, at the bottom of which foam the heavy waves of the Atlantic. At some spots a workman pushes along a narrow path, or even along a fragile plank, a little truck loaded with stones, taking advantage of the steep inclines to save his strength. On the edge of a yawning abyss is a pool of water, reddened by oxide of tin, in which men and lads are standing up to their knees. This liquor afterwards runs into the sea; we might call it the blood of the mines; and it colours the waves for a very considerable distance, thus adding a red belt to the belts of foam and dark green which break hoarsely on the beach. This coast is savage, but the miners appear so familiarized with the stern beauties of nature, that when their work is ended they go to take the air and sun themselves in the gorges of Pornamra Head, a rude promontory, straight as a wall, to which you are obliged to cling with feet and hands.

The Levant Mine offers at certain spots an even more formidable appearance. There, in the rock gorges which yawn as if to defy all communication, the workmen have succeeded in forming a passage from one point to another, along clumsy viaducts suspended betwixt heaven and sea. And yet, in spite of the dangers, in spite of these accumulated horrors, what a scene of movement and activity!

Of all the mines called submarine, because they extend beneath the bed of the Atlantic, the one which most attracts tourists and curious people is Botallack Mine. In the book in which visitors write their names I found the signatures of the Duc d'Aumale, Prince de Joinville, and the Comte de Paris. Persons at the spot still remember having seen them descend the shaft in mining dresses and with tools, and emerge covered with mud, and carrying lumps of tin and copper which they had themselves quarried. The Botallack Mine employs upwards of 600 workmen, who toil, some on the surface, others in the interior of the earth, along a coast bristling with rocks and beaten by the fury of the winds and waves. In nature, as in art, there are beauties that terrify, and such is the character of this seaboard.

In the midst of precipices which produce a dizziness, it is a grand sight to see man, that weak being, only strong in the power of his brain, preparing to conquer and subdue the blind turbulence of the elements. The wind whistles round his head, the earth falls, as it were, beneath his feet, the waves yawn at an immense depth to swallow him; but he does not tremble. He descends by steep paths, by tottering wooden steps, by straight and steep ladders. Whither is he going? Beneath the face of the rocks, doubtless. Lower, much lower still. He is going under the sea, under that mighty abyss of water, whose heavy shingle he can hear distinctly above his head. A band of these bold miners one day found in the submarine galleries a fine piece of copper which was only three feet beneath the water. With that contempt of danger which characterizes men of their profession, they attacked the roof of the mine, dug a hole in it, and filled it up with mortar.

Some of the subterranean galleries run for more than half a mile under the sea. In order to descend to these gloomy passages, it was naturally necessary to dig shafts along the coast, and these shafts are covered with white engine-houses, scattered along the summits or slopes of the black rocks whose irregular surface resembles the gnarled bark of an old tree. In order to convey the ore out of the mine to the stamping works, it has also been necessary to form wooden galleries with tramways, along which small carts run. Such works thrown over abysses are certainly of a nature to confound the imagination. How could they possibly have been carried out? How can they be kept up? These structures, of a relatively fragile character, seem at every instant as if they would be crushed by the enormous masses of rock hanging over them. Man, however, does not always spurn danger with impunity. At the time when I visited Botallack, the memory of a rather recent catastrophe still hung like a cloud over the sublime horrors of this mine. Nine men and a boy were mounting from the underground works in a tram-waggon, when, just as they had reached the surface, a chain broke, and they were all precipitated into eternal night. Such accidents, however, do not subdue the temerity of the miners; and in spite of disasters perhaps inevitable, who would not admire at Botallack Mine the grandeur of industry associated with the grandeur of nature?

Not satisfied with introducing themselves by winding roads beneath the ocean bed, some years ago the adventurers carried their audacity much farther. Close to Penzance, in a deep bay which waters the charming esplanade, they opened the mouth of a mine in the very midst of the waves. This mine, known by the name of Wherry Mine, had been begun 720 feet from the beach, and the labourers worked 100 feet under water. The entrance of the shaft was in the centre of the bay, and at each recurrent tide it was surrounded by the boiling waves. The upper part of the shaft consisted of a caisson, which rose twelve feet above the level of the sea, and standing amid the rubble which had been taken out of the bowels of the mine. The miners thus descended through the water to the scene of their subterranean labours; the water continually dripped, and fell drop by drop from the roof of the galleries, while they distinctly heard above their heads the thunder of the waves. A steam-engine was erected on the shore; by the aid of pipes it communicated with the interior of the shaft, and thus pumped out the water which ran into the bay. These pipes passed along a platform supported by pillars. One day it happened that a vessel driven by a storm dashed against this platform, and carried away a portion. The ore obtained by this bold enterprise was of good quality, but the cost of extraction was enormous, and gradually ate up the profits. The mine was therefore abandoned. It has, however, given its name to a suburb of the town, which is called to this day Wherry Town.

All the mines do not possess the same dramatic character. What the undertakers demand of them is not, as may be supposed, to supply inspiration to artists, but to pay good dividends. The richest are collected between Camborne and Redruth, on hills which rise three or four hundred feet above the level of the sea. At the foot of this chain of hills are fertile valleys, so that the land is divided, in a manner more or less unequal, between the farmers and miners. The gloomy barrenness of the soil is found, so to speak, by the side of the most dazzling verdure. The country itself is literally studded with cottages. These white houses, at times alone, at others distributed in groups of two or three, are solidly built of stone, and serve as residences for the Titans of the mines. The latter are very fond of getting away from the villages when they find a chance; this is a way of obtaining cheaply half an acre of land, which they convert into a field or garden. What most strikes the visitor in these mining districts, especially at certain hours of the day, is the solitude. Everything announces that the country is very populous, but where are the inhabitants? Underground. Along the roads and in the houses one only finds old women and little children.

Camborne and Redruth are two centres which owe all their importance to copper and tin. Fresh villages have sprung up as if by enchantment during later years; long rows of houses, all uniform, and looking at a distance like barracks, extend in different directions around the old nucleus of the town. These houses, as an Englishman said to me, are the mushrooms of the mine; they have grown there solely through the vicinity of the works. If you mount a hill, you discover all around you huge chimneys in the shape of obelisks, which are to the mines what masts are to vessels. Some are tin mines, others copper mines; most frequently they produce both metals.

There are some, again, which offer a character of grandeur and poetry, owing to their association with romantic scenery. Such is Carn-Brea Mine, situated near a bare and stern hill, crowned with immense flat rocks lying on each other, whose origin antiquarians refer to the ancient Druids, and geologists to natural convulsions. Near the top, a large serrated rock is, according to the old traditions of the country, the petrified hand of a giant, who at a single stride reached St. Agnes, situate four miles from Carn-Brea. Leaving the fabulous for the reality, we will proceed to Dolcoath Mine, near Camborne, where we shall be enabled to study closely the character of the excavations and the series of metallurgical labours.

This mine, now one of the most flourishing, and which yields to its shares a million of profit, was regarded during a long time as exhausted. Everybody despaired of it, and the shares had fallen to nothing, when they were so lucky as to find a vein of extraordinary wealth. These vicissitudes are not rare in the fortunes of mines. Botallack was equally abandoned. Other curious alternatives are also met with. Dolcoath Mine was for a while extremely rich in copper; at the present day it only yields tin: it is true that the galleries then ran through slate rock, while now they penetrate the granite. Piercing granite was formerly regarded as an impossible, or at the least an unproductive, enterprise; but at present the mining art recognizes no obstacles. The works are situated close to the town, in a melancholy and open country: it is supposed that trees, perhaps even forests, formerly grew there, but that they were burned to melt the metal at a period when coal was not employed.

I was first introduced into the committee-room. Nearly all the copper and tin mines belong to companies. When some individuals believe they have found mineral at any spot, and succeed in making others share their convictions, they generally form a company, which issues shares in order to raise the capital. These companies are subject, especially at the outset, to all the market changes. Those of the Great Devon Consols, which have paid enormous dividends for many years, were depreciated at first; no one would have them. I also know an inhabitant of Cornwall who might have made a fortune if he had merely lent his name to a company, which offered him in exchange pieces of paper, which have now a value of several thousand pounds. These transactions have entirely the character of a lottery; some attain to wealth by them, others are ruined. The mining share-market offers, in Cornwall, the strangest variations; and it is not rare to see these securities vary from 200 to 300 per cent. in a week. Frequently, when a mine fails, the heads of the undertaking, who have an interest in getting rid of their shares, try to raise a belief in a fictitious prosperity. The best lumps of ore, which have been held in reserve for the occasion, are then brought up the shaft, as if the miners had just struck a new vein. Wise men are suspicious, and call this, in the language of the country, "tearing the eyes out of the mine."

In the committee-room I saw maps that admirably indicated the plan and internal structure of a mine. There is a perfect subterranean geography for the whole district: the limits of these black kingdoms are clearly traced, with the extent and depth of each mine, the number of shafts, the names of the lodes, and the direction of the galleries, which have never seen the light of day. The interior of the earth is as well divided as the surface. It is the principle of the English law that all metalliferous soil belongs to the Crown, unless it abandons this privilege, as it does in Cornwall, to the landowner. Before opening a mine, the adventurers (the significative name given to the undertakers) have to pay what is called a royalty. This due is paid either to the Prince of Wales, as Duke of Cornwall, if the ore is under a common, or, in the contrary case, to the owner of the land whose subsoil it is proposed to invade. The royalty varies greatly, according to circumstances; but it generally consists of an agreed share of the ore which will be afterwards discovered. This done, the works begin.

What is proposed in opening a mine is to reach in the bosom of the earth, that is to say, in the cracks and fissures of the rocks, the metallic veins, which in Cornwall run east or west. For this purpose, a perpendicular shaft is first sunk to a depth of about sixty feet. Galleries, called levels, are next made. The tracing of these galleries is determined by the well-known direction of the veins; one gang of miners, therefore, work eastward, while another excavates westward, so as to form two tunnels. When a hundred yards have thus been opened, an obstacle presents itself in the want of air. This obstacle has been foreseen: hence two other gangs of labourers set to work in digging from the surface two other shafts, which will form and ventilate the two first subterranean galleries. By this system the levels can be continued to any length, the only conditions being to open an air-shaft every hundred yards. Mines, however, cannot be extended indefinitely; *en route* they meet with an insurmountable difficulty in the borders of the other mines surrounding them. As they cannot extend laterally, they must necessarily become deeper. A third gang of labourers returns to the original shaft, generally called the engine-shaft, and sink it sixty feet lower in the ground. Here the construction of tunnels or levels is continued, on the same principle as we have indicated, and the second subterranean floor receives, like the first, air by means of shafts sunk at regular distances. This second level is often followed by a third, and even a fourth: who can say when the depths of the shafts will stop? It was this assemblage of works, increased and multiplied during many years, that I went to visit at Dolcoath Mine.

A mine is a being: it lives, it works, it breathes; the shafts are its lungs; the pump-pipes its circulating system; it eats coal, which is thrown to it by tons; it has a name, a personality, a sex.

The English, who have not, like us, in their language, a masculine and feminine for inanimate things, but who range all in a neutral gender, have made an exception in favour of the mine, as they had already done for the ship. *She* is a woman, a sort of dark Proserpine, with features possessing a stern and glacial beauty. The miners speak of her with respect: she kills them, and they love her. She is for them the mysterious power of good and evil. She tears out her entrails to enrich the human race; she daily enlarges her wounds, whence flow tin and copper; but she has poisoned blasts which shorten the miner's life, and abysses that swallow him up. Of all the organs which strike and amaze the traveller in the gigantic mechanism of a Cornish mine, the most remarkable is the pump-engine. Endowed with colossal stature and strength, it seeks the water at extraordinary depths; and yet this high-pressure engine is so admirably docile, that it can be managed by a child's hand. It occupies an elegant room, kept as clean as a lady's boudoir. By means of a species of clock, the counter, it will itself mark the number of its strokes, and thus indicate the amount of work it performs. The result of these calculations is published once a month in the local papers. In order to understand the utility of such machines, without which no working would be possible, or at least no deep working, it must be known that the mine is, in the language of a Cornish poet, a desolate widow, who sheds eternal tears. These tears, dropping continually from the roofs and pillars, speedily collect in pools, in lukewarm and dusky ponds. If this water were not got rid of by mechanical processes, the whole mine would be eventually drowned.

The amount of this subterranean water varies with the nature of the country; in the neighbourhood of Camborne, where the district is subjected to continual drainage, it is less than at other spots. It must not be supposed, however, that the pumps bring all this water to the surface; there are mines which only collect the quantity necessary for their consumption; there are others, like Dolcoath, which apply to a neighbouring stream to water their external works. Raising the water to such a height is an enormous expense, and science, agreeing with economy, has suggested to the mining engineers other means of getting rid of it. In such a case a level is sought, where the dead water can escape spontaneously into a river or the sea. Such openings or trenches are called adits. The function of the pump in such a case is to draw the water towards these artificial conduits. It frequently happens that such works present a stupifying character of boldness. The great adit, which receives the waters of several mines in the Gwennap and Redruth districts, runs, counting its ramifications, for a distance of more than thirty miles, and at some spots it is 400 feet below the surface of the ground. The principal branch is alone five and a half miles in length, and falls into the sea at Restronget Creek. Such works, if I am not mistaken, will furnish a very great idea of Cornwall.

These waters, drawn from the bottom of the mines, impart a singular appearance to the whole district; they may be easily recognized by their colour. At some places, for instance at Helston, I saw them running along both sides of the street in stone conduits, where they form streams to clean and refresh the town. They even form rivers and lakes. At a mile from Helston there is a damp and greasy meadow through the middle of which runs a brick-coloured current, whose sediment stains the grass. This current swells and falls into a lake, Looeport, surrounded by sand-banks which are entirely submerged in the floods.

The surface of the port, which is about seven miles in circumference, ripples and is agitated, and the waves are violently raised upon it by the fresh breeze coming from the sea. Gradually the country rises and is covered on the right by a wood, in which is the charming estate of Mr. Rogers, M.P. This foliage forms a picturesque contrast with the red hue of Looeport, on whose surface float white swans. You leave the wood by a steep path that winds between rocks, and soon find yourself facing one of the most extraordinary sights in nature. At the end of the lake is the sea, from which it is only separated by a sand-bank, called the Bar. This strip of fine sand is about two hundred paces in width, and closes all communication between the sea and Looeport. While walking along the bar, you have in front of you the ocean—a green, dark mass, with a fringe of foam, and behind you the lake, which *en route* has slightly changed its colour. It is now a pink shot with silver. This contrast is striking; here calmness, or at the most a ripple, there the dark abyss on which storms are engendered. Looeport, however, is not always so tranquil. It frequently happens, especially in winter, that, owing to the mass of water descending from the hills, and filtering into the sea through the sand-bank, the port swells, overflows, stops the working of the mills, and inundates the roads and the lower part of the town. In such a case, the corporation of Helston go to the lord of the manor (Mr. Rogers) and, according to a very old custom, give him a copper purse containing three half-pennies; at the same time they ask leave to cut the bar. When this has been done, the workmen begin; a small trench is opened in the sand, which is soon widened by the violence of the stream, and an immense river rushes into the sea, though not without waging a terrific combat with the powerful waves that repel it. The tumultuous passage of all this water, I was told, is a strange and grand scene, especially on a moon-lit night. The mass of it reaches as far as the Scilly isles, being known by the red colour of the sea. The cut bar is repaired at the end of a few days by the sand which the ocean washes up, especially in stormy weather. The sea, like liberty, sets bounds on itself.

To return to Dolcoath Mine. The workmen at these great undertakings have two perfectly distinct operations to perform; these are the underground and the ground works. Let us first occupy ourselves with the former, which offer a peculiar interest through the dangers connected with them. Dolcoath Mine is 2,000 feet in depth. It spreads over a superficies of three quarters of a square mile, and one of its branches passes under the railway. There are none deeper, but many more extensive; the consolidated mines run sixty-three miles under ground! You descend into the interior most usually by ladders fastened to the side of the shaft; but at Dolcoath, and a few other mines, there is a man-engine, a sort of moving staircase, which excellent invention was suggested a few years ago by the Falmouth Polytechnic Society. Any one who wishes to visit the black regions of a mine, were he the Prince of Wales himself, must first put on the miner's dress. This consists of canvas trousers, a jacket lined with thick flannel, and a round hat, a regular helmet, intended to protect the skull against the stones and lumps of rock that fall here and there from the roof. Every miner has in a common room a large wooden trunk, in which he locks up his tools and clothes, and whence he takes his working dress before entering the mine. Thus accoutred, with a candle fixed on the brim of the hat in a lump of soft clay, and a packet of candles fastened to a button hole, he speedily disappears in the mouth of the shaft. He descends from level to level until he reaches the vein in which he is at work.

The interior of the copper or tin mines is very melancholy. You walk in them, sometimes upright, sometimes bent, sometimes even you crawl, according to the height of the roof. In these solitudes, where you fancy you can hear the dull buzzing of night in your ears, you find at regular distances the athletic sons of Cornwall in the strangest and most impossible attitudes; by the weak light of the candles they look like the caryatides of the mines. These gloomy passages, however, do not bear for the miners that character of sepulchral horror which produces such a profound impression of melancholy on a stranger's mind. They merely complain of the height of the temperature and the stagnant air they breathe in certain low and contracted spots. In those mines that run beneath the sea, the heat is sometimes so great and the air so compressed, that the miners throw buckets of water over their bodies to refresh them and be enabled to continue their labour. Accidents are frequent and terrible; they most usually result from the fall of blocks which become detached and crush the miners; at other times the foot slips on the fatal ladders, or else the powder suddenly explodes in the face of the miners at the moment when they imagined the charge had failed. At St. Just, I met in the streets at least a dozen of blind and disfigured miners.

Among these accidents there are some doubtless inevitable, but also some that might easily be prevented. Some useful reforms have been lately introduced; the ladders have been shortened, and rendered less perpendicular; and platforms have been established, so that the men may rest. To what rude trials this mode of ascent puts human strength, will be comprehended when we learn that the workmen frequently take an hour in ascending from the bottom of the mine to the surface. The improvements unfortunately meet with an obstacle in the power of routine, and too often in the parsimony of the shareholders. The man-engine, that most advantageous substitute for ladders, costs about £1,200 to fit up, for a shaft must be made expressly for it, and often the richest undertakings refuse to make such an outlay. Accidents caused by gunpowder and the fall of rocks might also be alleviated by recent inventions, which I found but too rarely employed in the Cornish mines.

The miners remain six or eight hours under ground. Their task—and it is a hard one—naturally consists in digging out the metal and separating it from the rock that contains it. While the men are thus breaking the masses of slate or granite, enormous buckets, called kibbles, slide heavily along chains, and convey the produce of the works to the surface by all the mouths of the mine, which are most usually seven or eight in number. At the end of this time the first gang of miners has finished what is called a round, and is relieved by fresh hands. In the works where the men go on for eight hours there are consequently three successive rounds of miners every twenty-four hours. The mine never rests, and some men indeed prefer working at night; it is true that night is of the same colour as day in these gloomy passages. At the moment when the men collect to go up, some moving groups of lighted candles may be seen in the dark corners and passages. With the miners, returning to the surface is returning to grass. They are then seen emerging one by one, pale, covered with perspiration, and thirsting for fresh air. With what joy do they inhale the first breath of the breeze that expands their lungs! And yet the sudden change of atmosphere, this transition from the hot and stagnant air to a sharp breeze, especially during cold frosty nights, is frequently the source of mortal diseases. With hands, face, and clothes covered with a reddish earth, they run for a wash to a basin filled with lukewarm water that always flows abundantly from the steam-engine. A few minutes after they have changed their appearance, and walk slowly toward their cottages.

Examples of longevity must not be sought among the miners. On the average, they do not live beyond forty years. Mr. Hadow, the vicar of St. Just, thus told me the melancholy result of his observations and experience: "I have seen," he said, "many widows among the miners, but not a single widower." Those who are not killed by accident perish of exhaustion and excessive toil; the rock is so hard and the ladders are so long. Very admirable is the stoical coldness with which they regard their fate. Cornwall is proud, and justly so, of her miners. Who can say what England owes to these men? They produce riches, and scarcely enjoy common necessaries themselves.

Among the miners, some are on piece-work, others on what is called tribute. The meaning of these two words must be explained. When a mine is opened, it is all piece-work, that is to say, so much a fathom is paid. Afterwards, when the mine has begun to yield, the same arrangements are continued; but there is also another mode of payment which is a real improvement on the usual system of wages.

In addition to the piece-workmen, here called tutmen, there are the tributers. The latter have no settled rate of wages, but undertake the work at their own risk and peril. The interior of the mine is left open for the inspection of all the miners who live in the neighbourhood, and each compartment or pitch is allotted by auction to two or four men. This arrangement only lasts for two months, and at the expiration of that period the works are again put up to competition. The reason for so short a lease is the uncertainty such undertakings offer. The veins of metal appear and disappear. As a clever engineer said to me, "They resemble those black veins we see crossing marble, and which vanish all at once. Who knows to what depth and in what direction they must be followed?" The nature and density of the rock also change at certain depths; hence there is a concourse of chances which entirely defy calculation. The tributer may dig for months without finding ore, while he may have the luck to fall on a very rich vein after a few days. Sometimes, too, an originally rich vein suddenly grows poor, or else it takes the bit in its teeth, as they say here, that is to say, it breaks off and disappears in the interior of the rock. The result is that the earnings of the tributers are subject to the strangest variations, from 1s. to 200l. or 300l. per month. It is evident that I give the two ends of the scale, but the degrees are very uneven. The tributer's share of the quantity of metal he raises also differs considerably, according to the ground and the nature of the works. We see from this that the tributer's life is exposed to much disappointment, and often to reverses which swallow up his labour and his small savings; and yet his situation, compared with that of the other miners, has something princely about it. He is to a certain extent a partner in the profits of the mine; he is his own master; and if, after all, he does not earn more than another man, he heightens by this mode of payment that which man justly places far above large profits—his dignity. Unfortunately the adventurers only employ tributers in bad veins; the better ones are excavated by miners on piece-work.

The ground works have a very different character from those that take place in the interior of the mine. Their business is to prepare for trade the mineral torn from the bowels of the earth. If the ore is copper, and rich in metal, the labour is greatly simplified; if, on the other hand, it is tin, this has to be got out by a series of operations. In either case the task is intrusted to women and children. These works are carried on partly in the open air, partly in wooden sheds, which are worth visiting. The different and successive processes consist of breaking, pounding, washing, and burning the mineral. It is broken with hammers by women, or, if it prove too hard, by men. The women are remarkable for a peculiar head-dress—a pasteboard foundation covered with a piece of gaudy calico, fastened on the head by means of ribbons, while large wings fall and float round the face. Such an apparatus serves at once as bonnet, cap, and veil; it admirably protects the face from the sun; and the mining girls are very anxious to retain their ruddy complexion.

The second process, or crushing the mineral, is performed by the stamping machine. Heavy perpendicular beams, succeeding each other in line like organ pipes, fall one after the other with enormous force, and pulverize the tin mixed with the rock. The noise of the machine is deafening; in the mines situated near the seashore, it is the only one that can contend with the voice of the waters. The mineral is now a powder; but this powder is far from being pure. In order to separate the tin from the damp dust of the rock, various washing processes are employed. This third operation is far more complicated than the two others. Water is naturally the principal agent in the works; it forms here and there reservoirs, in which, mixed with oxide of tin that turns it red, it is constantly agitated by rakes, brooms, and other implements in female hands.

One of the most interesting processes is what is called framing or racking. The hand-frame exactly resembles one of those old wooden beds which may still be met with in hospitals and barracks. It is composed of a frame, the bottom being a large plank, shaped like a table, and placed at an inclined plane. The mineral powder is laid on what I will call the bed head; the water is set flowing, and carries off with it all this matter; the workwoman then brings back the tin to the top of the plank, and spreads it over the upper part by means of a flat rake. The metal eventually is deposited through its weight, while the muddy water escapes at the bottom, and falls into a receptacle. When this has been done, the table turns on its axis and falls over on its side, and the deposited metal, which alone remains, is driven by water into boxes intended to receive it. The other machines, though very numerous and varied, are all applications of the same natural law, that of specific gravity. As tin is the heaviest body of all those treated in the mining works, practical science has taken advantage of this circumstance to collect it and liberate it from foreign matter.

The mineral has still a final heat to undergo—calcination. It is burnt in ovens, whence escapes a white smoke, indicating the presence of arsenic. The walls themselves distil the poison; the air is loaded with it. Men, their clothes all loaded with a greyish dust so fatal to animal life, and with a pocket-handkerchief pressed to their lips, pass like shadows before the mouth of the furnace. Near the burning-house, in the midst of fumes and piles of arsenic, I, however, saw a pretty girl, whose bright colour and look of flourishing health seemed to defy these pernicious influences. After all, poisons have their value; the arsenic is very carefully collected, and is then sold for a pound the ton. At the end of the sheds I at length found a heap of mineral, which was the result of all the previous operations, and which was sufficiently prepared for trade. During the process it had slightly changed colour; it had become brown through the action of the fire. This heap was worth £1,000.

Dolcoath Mine employs 1,300 persons, 500 under ground and 800 on the surface. These labourers, male and female, are paid once a month. All the moralists of Cornwall condemn this system of payment at long intervals, which forms such a painful contrast with the habit generally adopted in England of paying the workman the fruit of his labour every week. I witnessed the payment of wages at Botallack Mine; the office table was literally covered with gold: nearly £1,500 would be dispersed within a few hours. Very little of this golden shower, however, falls into the hand of each: a miner's great wage averages seventeen shillings a week. The day of payment is at the same time the one on which what may be called the sale of the works for the following month takes place. The general manager proceeds to a window, the upper sash of which has been let down, and mounting a chair, he thence addresses the miners, who have remained in the open air. With a list in his hand he reads aloud the prices which have been asked by the miners for so many fathoms, and how much the mine is disposed to offer them. The reduction is generally very considerable, but is nearly always accepted. The miners are perfectly well aware that they will meet with the same conditions elsewhere.

The mineral, which we have seen prepared at the works, soon leaves the sheds for a fresh scene of operations. If it is tin, it is purchased by the tin smelting works. The most important of these is Mr. Bolitho's, at Penzance. Here the mineral, which has been brought in heavy waggons, is subjected to an examination, and paid for according to its value; it then passes through a fresh series of most interesting operations, until it becomes metal.

Cornwall produces monthly about 1,300 tons of tin, which are reduced by smelting to 850 tons of metal, and represent an annual capital of a million. The tin smelted in Cornwall is conveyed to Wales and Staffordshire, where it is made into plates, and applied to the different wants of trade.

Copper, on the other hand, is first sold at Redruth or Truro, according to a peculiar system, to which the name of ticketing has been given. In a room set apart for the purpose, the quantity of mineral which has reached the market that day is announced, as well as its quality, which has been determined by experiments made beforehand on samples. The bidders, collected round a table, silently write their offers on a slip of paper, which they fold up and deposit in a glass. A clerk of the ticketings then opens them, and proclaims the highest bidder, to whom the mineral is adjudged. This, it will be seen, is a sort of sale by auction, but conducted in the most perfect silence. The result of the scrutiny, that is to say, the price, is published the next day in the newspapers. The copper thus bought is afterwards sent by water to Wales, principally to Swansea, where there are immense copper-smelting works. The reason why the copper is not smelted in Cornwall is because that county does not contain coal.

The west of England most certainly owes the greater part of its wealth to the presence of metals; but what would be the capital sleeping in the earth, without the energy and skill of the miners? The Cornish miners are a select race; at the first glance you can distinguish them from the farm labourers, for they are so greatly noted by their stature and by an air of reflection and self-confidence. This physical and moral superiority results from the nature of their work, which develops their strength, but exercises the judgment still more, as well as all the mental faculties. The children of the miners generally attend school till the age of ten or twelve. After that age they enter the mine, where they at first work on the surface, and when they have become adult and strong, they gradually descend under ground. At the end of some time they know the value of ores, and the manner of finding them, as well as scientific men. It has been said of the Cornish miners that they possess the mathematics of the mole. Endowed with a species of instinct, and an admirable judgment, they find means practically to solve certain problems which seem to demand all the calculations of geometry. What height would this penetration attain if it were aided by study? Unfortunately, this is a question difficult to answer, for when they have set foot in a mine, they have only, to complete a most imperfect education, the night and Sunday schools. In the latter they learn to read the Bible. Some years ago Mr. Robert Hunt, of the Practical Geology Museum, established in Cornwall a miners' association, whose members can attend lectures on chemistry, mineralogy, and geology. This institution renders some service, but meets with obstacles in certain prejudices intrenched behind ignorance and routine.

When at home, the miner employs himself

more or less in his garden, in which he cultivates flowers and vegetables. His house, which he often builds with his own hands, is not at all bad looking. Its furniture is plain; but you generally find in it two things which constitute the pride of an English home—stairs covered with a neat carpet, and very clean windows hung with curtains. Towards strangers he is kind and hospitable, though he is rough and rather coarse in his manner. His mode of living is extremely temperate; he never eats meat except on holidays. It is impossible to form an idea of a miner's kitchen without entering one. In the sheds at Dolcoath Mine there is a room in which the miners dry their clothes, and cook their dinner in an oven. This dinner consists of a turnip-pie, or a little quantity of flour and currants mixed together and browned with a red-hot plate. Along the coast the miners add fish to this frugal fare.

Having coolly looked on the mine and its horrors, they do not tremble at the sea. They catch their winter stock themselves in frail boats. They salt the fish—most frequently large conger eels—and hang it from the ceiling to dry: it is the bacon of these cottages.* With all this, they are tolerably contented with their lot; if their

---

* In the neighbourhood of St. Just some miners also have recourse to another method for increasing their domestic comfort: they have a cow, or *half a cow*; that is to say, the milk is divided between two families, who milk the cow in turn.

fare is poor, they have but few wants, and then they enjoy an advantage inestimable in their sight —independence. Sleeping little, at work most generally in the night hours, they walk about during the day either alone or with their wives; they might easily be taken for artists. Paid according to what they do, having a contract which determines the nature and extent of their work, they only acknowledge one master—duty. If they wish to emigrate, the whole world is open to them. In California, Australia, New Zealand, wherever there are mines, you meet with Cornish miners. In the time of the gold fever, the town of Camborne was suddenly nearly deserted, and workmen had to be fetched from Ireland. If, besides, labour alone does not enrich the miner, the same is not precisely the case with labour joined to speculation. The great Cornish fortunes have issued from the bottom of the mines, and many an ex-workman is now a rich landowner.

The life of the miners would not be thoroughly understood if we neglected their wives. The girls, like the boys, enter the works in the flower of their age. Their task is, as we have seen, to break and prepare the mineral. Wielding the hammer and the rake expands their shoulders and develops their form; hence they are generally well made, and are aware of the fact. At the time of their daily avocations they are clean and neatly dressed; if by accident any of them have shoes uncleaned, they hide them with a shamefaced look under their too short skirts when a stranger visits the works. When they leave the mine they repair hastily but artistically the disorder which washing the mineral has produced in their toilette; they then go across the fields in groups. These groups offer many contrasts—the girls laugh, sing, and teaze the lads; the children play; while the old miners walk in silence and with an absent air, thinking of their supper. As they pass the cottages built along the roadside the joyous band naturally grows smaller, and those who live farther from the mine continue their walk in solitude.

The girls have worked all day for a very small wage, generally seven or eight pence. Sometimes this money is honourably employed to support an old mother, or else proportionately to augment the comfort of the family; but only too often this small sum is used to satisfy coquetry. In vain do the parents strive to combat this fatal inclination: the girls leave the cottage plainly dressed, but under the nearest hedge they take out of their pocket a veil, a brooch, or some other ornament. The workwomen of the mines have an inveterate foe in the packman. This name is given to a pedlar who sometimes sells everything—sugar, tea, coffee, but more especially feminine finery. As he comes back every fortnight, he is also called, in familiar language, Johnny Fortnight. This man tempts the girls in their weak point, vanity. As he does not ask for cash payments, and on the contrary is satisfied with a small instalment every fortnight or month, the bargain is soon concluded. What is the use of being pretty if some expense is not incurred in helping and heightening nature? If a girl is on the eve of marriage, the packman persuades her that she wants a wedding outfit. She can pay this debt hereafter out of her husband's wages, and the transaction will be kept secret, for Johnny Fortnight represents himself as a model of discretion. It is always the same story, the compact of the maiden who sells herself to the fiend. From this day, in reality, she falls into the power of this man, who threatens to reveal everything if she does not keep her engagements, or refuses the goods he offers her afterwards. It is true that the miners, on their side, have recourse to the same means to procure their Sunday clothes. In Cornwall the Sunday is to the other days of the week what in English pantomimes the transformation scene is. You cannot recognize the ordinary mining population: underground grubs during the week, and butterflies in the Sunday sun. On this day the men wear black coats, their wives silk dresses and bonnets with flowers. After all, is this tendency blameable? Elegance being one of the fruits of civilization, everybody desires to acquire it, as an external sign of an honourable and laborious life. The English only understand an equality that aspires and wishes to rise; to this they make great sacrifices: hence, in spite of the profound differences of rank and fortune, Great Britain is the country in which dress is most uniform and makes the nearest approach to luxury.

The Cornish mines are a continually increasing source of wealth for the United Kingdom. The English attribute this wealth to the nature of the subsoil, but also in great part to the system of free working by companies. I am bound to say they profess but slight admiration for the French mining system, which is impeded by regulations and guiding reins. It is not that they do not allow that the pupils of the French mining schools possess great learning and talent, but they charge the State with interfering too much, and thus exerting a fatal pressure on the spirit of initiation and the moral resources of the country. Our excellent system, with the ordinary service, the extraordinary service, and the detached system, does not at all tempt them. They also say that the hand of authority is seen too much above all these wheels, and they cannot sufficiently distinguish the action of individuals, or the impulsive force of associated capital. What would you have? These unfortunate

English do not understand the blessings of a paternal government. Believing themselves strong enough to manage their own affairs, they have thrown off the protection of the State, and setting vigorously to work, they have forced the bowels of the earth to enrich them. If we were to judge of the two systems by the result, as the Gospel bids us to judge of the tree by its fruit, we could not hesitate to decide in favour of the latter. Self-government applied to the mining profession has produced in Cornwall incomparable fortune; it supplies work for 15,000 or 20,000 hands, and has converted a slip of land which nature had treated in a step-motherly way, into a horn of abundance for Great Britain.

CHAPTER III.

BRIXHAM—PRESENT STATE OF THE TOWN AND PORT—THE FISHING-BOATS—THE MARKET—THE LORDS OF THE MANOR—HOME MISSIONARIES — FISHERMEN'S WIVES — NETS — GENERAL OPINION ABOUT THE TRAWL—CLEMENT PINE—ANNE PERRIAM—DISTRESS AT SEATON—DIFFERENCE BETWEEN THE DEVON AND CORNISH FISHERIES.

ENGLAND owes a great part of her wealth to her sea-board; she is also indebted to it for natural beauties which have often been celebrated by poets and novelists. Only to speak here of the south-west coast, it would be difficult to find elsewhere such a series of landscapes, equally grand and exquisite in turn. The English, who do not cultivate art for the sake of art, have not failed to take advantage of these picturesque sites. In these deep bays, full of deep water, they have built towns and formed ports which attract, and to some extent invite, all the vessels of the world; other and narrower bays, but not the less interesting for the landscape-painter, were occupied at an early period by fishermen. During the last century, however, this land has been torn from them to a great extent. Sumptuous watering-places have deposed the fishing villages, which are now driven into the background and hidden by rich terraces, newly-built crescents and esplanades, bounded by magnificent buildings. The sea is the great physician of the English; of it they ask health, restoration of strength, and mental rest after a year of fatigue. It is thus that Sidmouth, Exmouth, Dawlish, Teignmouth, Torquay, Ilfracombe, and other towns in Devon, responding to this imperious want, have become, in spite of their considerable distance from London, the great rendezvous for those who have not stopped at Hastings or Brighton. In these modern cities—which have to some extent risen from the bosom of the sea, with their bold cliffs surmounted by villas and palaces—wealth, fashion, and pleasure have during the last few years given a really marvellous impulse to trade. In this way a brilliant centre has been formed, in which no attention is paid to the fishermen.

Still, it is to this class of simple men, who are courageously useful and too often victims to the perfidious beauties of the sea, that I now wish to call attention. Between these and the miners a sort of family likeness may be noticed; both classes frequently live in the same villages, connected by the bond of dangers, by austere duties, and by simple manners which command respect. The fishery on the western coast possesses peculiar features which it is important to study in turn: the character of the rocks on which the hamlets stand, the nature of the nets, and, last, the species of fish that visit the shore. Among the latter there is one which belongs to Cornwall—the pilchard. With this obscure inhabitant of the seas, which is but little known even in England, a very considerable branch of trade is connected, which supplies entire populations with bread and work.

Before entering Cornwall, I stopped at Brixham, an old fishing town situated on the coast of Devonshire, near Torbay. Nestling in a valley which opens on the sea, it forms a long parallelogram commanded by lofty cliffs of coarse limestone, rich in iron ore, which is daily extracted. The houses, which are too restricted in this nook, and extend for nearly a mile, have necessarily spread in the course of time over the surrounding hills which enclose the port. Some on the right and left are scattered over the heights: with their white walls and pointed roofs, they resemble in the distance aquatic birds perched on the brink of precipices. In order to reach them, streets had to be opened, that is to say, flights of steps formed in the rocks. One of these streets, which I scaled, had, if I counted correctly, 116 steps; it was cut at regular stages by terraces, also excavated in the rock, and bordered on one side by a parapet, on the other by the fishermen's cottages, clinging to the steep and almost perpendicular sides of the overhanging cliffs. These houses, which are whitewashed, look clean, but they are cold and bare; in front of them are small gardens without flowers. Such abodes share to some extent the rigidity of the rock on which they seem rooted. In default of shrubs and verdure you notice here and there on these patches of ground linen drying, or at times lines of dried fish supported in the air by long props. Everything here speaks of navigation and fishing. From the last terrace the eye surveys nearly the whole town of Brixham—a draughtboard of houses with narrow yards and stairs in the open air; but the eye dwells with preference on the port, which really offers an interesting scene.

This port is a large basin enclosed on the side of the town by quays substantially constructed of cut stone, and defended seaward by a strong pier, built in 1803. On its calm waters sleep the fishing-boats or smacks which for the moment are not employed. Ten years ago Brixham was one of the most flourishing fishing ports on the coast; but now it is in a state of decadence. The fish are retiring to deeper waters. At the period when I visited Torbay, another circumstance increased the consternation of the inhabitants. For the last twelve months the wind had been quite subdued; and with the system of nets adopted by the Brixham fishermen, nothing is caught when a

G

steady breeze is not blowing. This obstinate calm was displayed in fatal results. I saw in the port several bankrupt smacks, their owners had mortgaged them for more than they were worth, and now, seized by the creditors, dismasted, and obliged to remain on the beach, the poor smacks looked as sad as prisoners for debt in the Queen's Bench.

Such a painful state of inaction enabled me at least to inspect the boats at my leisure, and I found them composed of three principal compartments—a fore-cabin, in which the sails and rigging are stored; a hold, in which the fish is deposited; and a back cabin, in which the fishermen sleep. This last cabin is relatively very small, and surrounded by benches; the flat beds, covered with a rough brown counterpane, run along each side in narrow and dark bunks. The crew of a fishing-boat varies according to its size and importance, but is generally composed of three men and a boy. These smacks sometimes remain six days and six nights at sea, and proceed twenty or thirty miles from land. During the night one of the sailors remains on deck, while the three others sleep in the cabin. If the wind rises he warns his comrades, who at once get up and merrily throw the nets into the sea.

The smack usually belongs to a master, who supplies the crew with provisions, but deducts so much from the earnings of each man. The mode of payment is based on what the fishermen catch. It is a lottery, in which the wind and other natural chances play a great part in producing good and bad luck. Two tons of fish a trip is generally regarded as a good haul. This is divided into seven parts, of which four belong to the crew and three to the owner of the smack. The share of the crew is subdivided again according to the importance of the hands, the skipper receiving more than the mate, and the latter more than the third man. As for the boy, he receives 7s. a week, and is victualled by the owner. The division is made in money, and hence, before this can be done, the fish must be sold.

The market is held on the left hand of the port, at a spot paved with large slabs, and covered with an iron roof supported by heavy metal pillars. In the centre of this market-place was formerly shown the stone on which the Prince of Orange landed on Nov. 5th, 1688, when he came to England to dethrone the weak and despotic James II. As this stone impeded circulation, it has been removed to the centre of the pier, where it has been placed in a granite obelisk. The best time to see the Brixham fish-market is on Saturday evening; all the smacks that can find room enter the port, while the rest of the fleet anchors at the mouth of the bay. All sorts of *frutti del mare* are landed; soles, mullet, whiting, and monsters with glistening scales. The quay at this time offers an animated and picturesque scene; the piled-up fish, the women selling them by outcry, the men and women packing them in baskets, the carts waiting to convey them to the railway—all this, a few years ago, supplied the English painter Collins with the subject for a pretty picture. At the present day the number of smacks and trucks has unfortunately diminished; but the women who sell the fish by auction have retained a peculiar character, striking colours, masculine manners, as well as a decided taste for smart dresses and jewellery.

I conversed more than once with the groups of fishermen who walk up and down the quay with a gloomy and idle air. All deplore the decline of a trade which has been affected by causes difficult to discover. They are poor, but dignified. Among them I was introduced to one of the "lords" of Brixham. A lord in thick shoes, blue flannel shirt and trousers, with hands hardened by work and a face bronzed by the sea-breeze, was such a novel type of the English aristocracy that I opened my eyes in amazement. Some surprise was doubtless read on my countenance, for they began laughing, and one of the party explained to me the origin of this nobility. A quarter of the manor of Brixham was purchased some years ago by twelve fishermen. Since that time their shares have been divided and sub-divided, so that the title, or at least a portion of the title, has passed to a great number of families. These worthy people, who became manorial lords at a slight cost, are not the less treated with respect by their colleagues, who like to point them out to strangers.

Although a fisherman's life is more subject than any other to the accidents and reverses of fortune, these men, who have set their faith on the sea, neglect a great deal too much the provident institutions which exist for all other classes in Great Britain. They have certainly at Brixham sick and burial clubs, but they have not even a hospital. Everything is left, or nearly so, to chance, and to the charity of the poor towards the poor. They seem, in their simple faith, to have paid greater attention to the wants of the soul and to the duties of humanity than to material interests. On the side of one of the cliffs jutting farthest into the sea, a building is in course of construction, which is intended to serve as a school for the home missionaries, and a refuge for orphans. These missionaries are not destined to convert the savages, as their name implies; they will remain in their own country, and sow among their brethren the seed of the Gospel. They are sent to preach on board the vessels or smacks stationed in the bay. One of them having, in the opinion of the fishermen, offended propriety in his sermons, he was lately suspended. In order to avenge himself for this disgrace, and to display his zeal, he has built a new church on the point of one of the highest cliffs, which is most difficult of access. Possibly he wished his church to be reached by a strait and narrow way.

I expected to find among the wives of the English fishermen some of those characteristic costumes of which old Holland is so proud and jealous; but I met with a severe disappointment. With their hair smoothed on their temples, and fastened in a knot behind, the women of Brixham —dressed in short-sleeved black dresses, with flounced skirts—were not inferior in coquetry to the workwomen of London. Collected in groups, seated in front of the sea, on old sails, masts, or even chains and rusty anchors, they spend their time in knitting coarse blue woollen stockings. One of them, the poorest of all, as far as I could judge by appearances, had two children in her arms, twins. "If at least," she said, "Heaven had sent me three at once, the Queen would have sent me three guineas; but such good luck does not happen to Brixham women. Our town is condemned, the fish are going away, and children come a great deal too quick."

I must add that the population of Brixham, male and female, accept without discouragement the trials of evil fortune. And after all, the activity of the town has not relaxed. By the side of a ship-building yard, the sound of saws and hammers bears far along the waves the good news of work: a second arch is being made, in front of the first one, to shelter the vessels which now anchor in the open roads; the sail and net factories, which are principally served by women, are in a most flourishing condition. These nets, known by the name of trawls, impart a most peculiar character to the Devonshire fishery. The trawl is from thirty to seventy feet in length, and is in the shape of a bag. It is dragged along the bottom of the sea, and the mouth of the net, which is kept open by means of an ingenious mechanism, swallows up everything that comes in its way. Recently this system has been accused of having impoverished the sea, which is rapidly becoming depopulated. The Brixham fishermen themselves allow this in their simple language— the fish, they say, are not satisfied with them.

If the trawl has aroused detraction, it has also found advocates. It is not at all proved, as was first believed, that this apparatus, by sweeping the bed of the sea, destroys the fry; the instinct of the fish impels them to deposit their spawn on submarine rocks, and not on sand; and the fishermen carefully avoid venturing their nets among rocks, where they would inevitably be torn to pieces. The most serious fault to be found with the trawl is, that it devours, like the shark, with a blind and indiscriminating gluttony; the little fish, which would grow great if God granted their life, fare in it like the large ones. The remedy for this brutal and improvident destruction would be to enlarge the meshes of the net, so that the small fry could escape and grow at liberty till they were worth catching.

The Brixham fishermen form a race of bold adventurous men. One of them, Clement Price, went to the north of England to try his fortune. He began fishing there with a yawl he hired. Finding, however, fish scarce and luck bad, he had no hope of keeping his engagements, and returned the sloop to its owners. With two pounds—all the money left him—he bought a boat about fifteen feet in length, and got it ready himself for fishing; then he procured lines and hooks, hoping in this way to support himself and his family. In this he was once again deceived. Not knowing what to do, and not wishing to beg or steal, he resolved on returning to Brixham. Price consequently purchased some pounds of ship-biscuit, four pounds of salt pork, and a barrel of water; with this meagre provision he set sail. It was a long and perilous voyage, especially in an open boat. How could he keep awake day and night so as to turn the rudder of his frail boat in the proper direction? He certainly stopped *en route* at two or three ports; he even remained for some days on the coast to recruit his strength; but with the perseverance that characterizes the fishermen of Torbay, he put to sea again, and continued his voyage. Once, being assailed by a storm, he had one of his sails carried away by the wind. Nothing perturbed him; he merely altered his rigging, and soon ploughed once more through the raging waves, seeking his track across the abyss. Shortly after he put to sea, he found and picked up an old barrel; out of its iron hoops he constructed a grate, and with its wood he lit a fire to cook his food, after the fashion of Robinson Crusoe. Any one who had seen this man alone in the centre of the ocean, lost in the immensity of nature, and subduing it by the even more irresistible energy of his will, would doubtless have been moved to admiration. After a voyage of six hundred miles from North Sunderland to Brixham, he landed on July 9th, 1863, safe and sound, in the bay of his natal town. An inhabitant of St. Austel, in Cornwall, on hearing of this extraordinary voyage, offered Clement Price, in his own name and that of other generous persons, a fully-equipped sloop. A subscription was also opened to convert this sloop into a fishing-boat. "It would be a disgrace to the country," it was said, "for a man who has displayed such strength of character to be without the means of earning a livelihood."

The fishermen's wives also display at times that resolute temper which seems to be developed by commerce with the sea. At Exmouth, on this same coast of Devonshire, I paid a visit, in one of the poor quarters of the town, to an old fishwoman, Mrs. Anne Perriam, who was a heroine in her time. She was nineteen years of age when she married a sailor of the name of Hopping, who was serving on board the *Crescent*, a man-of-war commanded by Sir James Saumarez. After cruising for a long time off the French coast, this vessel was sent to Plymouth for repairs, and Anne Perriam was enabled to rejoin her husband. She even obtained leave to accompany him to sea. Some time after, Sir James was transferred from the *Crescent* to the *Orion*; Hopping and his wife followed him. For five years Mrs. Hopping served aboard this vessel, and took part in great naval battles. On June 23rd, 1795, she was at Lorient; on Feb. 14th, 1797, she was present at the action fought off Cape St. Vincent; on Aug. 1st, 1798, she saw the battle of the Nile won by Nelson: during the action her place was among the gunners and magazine keepers; she prepared cartridges for the heavy guns. Her brother fought aboard the same ship, with twelve other young men of Exmouth, all volunteers. One of these died an admiral. Anne Perriam is the only one who survives them: when I saw her, in 1863, she was ninety-three years of age. She had been twice married. After the death of her second husband, she obtained a livelihood by selling fish in the streets of Exmouth, her birthplace. Now, crushed by age, she appeared to me reduced to a state very nearly approaching to poverty. Her features evince a great strength of character: when you talk to her of the historic events which she witnessed, her face becomes animated, a proud smile flashes through her wrinkles, and her memory, which seems to be aroused by flashes, retraces with vivacity the story of the battles in which she formerly played the part of a man. Poverty, after a life of struggling and unknown exploits, is too frequently the reward of the English sailor and fisherman.

I also stopped at Seaton, near Axminster. This is a small fishing village which, when cheered by a sunbeam, conceals its indigence beneath the white cliffs and the blue mantle of the sea: in winter it is a sinister and lamentable spot. Winter is the bad season with fishermen; the ocean, covered with storms, contracts its entrails, if I may be allowed the expression, and refuses to support the inhabitants of the coast. At the beginning of 1864, Seaton, if I may trust letters I received, was sorely tried. The knell constantly tolled in the church tower, and five or six children were daily buried. Some of them died of small-pox; but the real, the most cruel malady of all, was hunger. The mothers ran about the village like wolves, and stoically witnessed the continuous funerals. A woman before whom the sad condition of her six children was pitied, as they sat there half clad and crouching round a dull fire of heath, answered; "Thank Heaven, they do not suffer so much as I, for I have nothing to give them. I should be glad to eat the wood of the table." In the midst of all this there was not a murmur or a tear; hunger seemed to have dried up all hearts and petrified all faces. Words of consolation, instead of soothing such suffering, only brought on nervous attacks. When persons said to the poor women, "Summer is coming, and Heaven will send us better days," they sobbed and fell into hysterical fits. In England, thank God, such calamities do not occur without soon becoming known, thanks to the liberty of the press; and then the almost inexhaustible sources of individual charity are opened. The fishermen of Seaton were the objects of effectual sympathy and help; but who will reach the root of the evil? The evil lies in the habit the population of the coast have of entirely trusting to the resources of the sea.

The trawl is the Devonshire net, and has given its name to the fishermen or trawlers. In Cornwall I was about to see a different apparatus—the drift net, or seine—as well as an entirely new coast formation. The limestone belt, after extending, with some interruptions, as far as Plymouth, gradually grows narrower as it runs to the west, and finally disappears in the centre of White Sand Bay. The whole region having been dislocated by old geological convulsions, it would be in vain to seek for that regular succession of strata which is met with in the other provinces of Great Britain, and represents the chronological series of courts. If there is a country which can be compared to Cornwall for the disorder of the rocks, it is Brittany, whose cliffs rise pell-mell on the other side of the Channel. These cataclysms, which have changed, rent, and at times even perverted the normal and primitive position of the ground, still imparts to Cornwall a character of grandeur and variety. This last characteristic is most visible in the belt of cliffs, a species of natural fortresses which have contended for centuries against the sea. Three systems of rock have given a peculiar imprint to the sea-board; serpentine, which prevails at Cape Lizard; granite, whose imposing features are chiefly developed at the Land's End; and the masses of slate, which have formed the wild promontories of Boscastle and Tintagel. Placed, I might almost venture to say imbedded, in these chains of cliffs, the fishing villages have more or less conformed their habits and mode of life to the nature of the country that surrounds them.

CHAPTER IV.

FABULOUS ORIGIN OF HELSTON—THE FIEND IN CORNISH LEGENDS—TREGEAGLE—THE FURRY—CAPE LIZARD—APPEARANCE OF THE CELTIC RACE—THE PRIMITIVE LANGUAGE OF CORNWALL—TRACES OF SPANISH ORIGIN—A FISHERMAN'S STORY—QUEEN ZENOBIA—ARE THE INHABITANTS OF CORNWALL DESCENDED FROM THE PHŒNICIANS?—LIZARD FISHERY COVE—KYNANCE COVE—THE PROMONTORIES AND ROCKS—THE CAVERNS—THE DEVIL'S FRYING-PAN—DOLOR HUGO—COMPOSITION OF THE ROCKS—SERPENTINE—THE LAND'S END—JOHN WESLEY AND TURNER—ARCHITECTURE OF THE ROCKS—DR. JOHNSON—SCUNEN—THE SCHOOL—SHIPWRECKS—THE FIRST AND LAST INN IN ENGLAND—THE THREE KINGS.

I WENT to Cape Lizard from Helston, a small town near the mines, in a semi-industrial, semi-agricultural district. If tradition may be believed, the name of this town sufficiently indicates that it owes its origin to the infernal regions. One day, says the legend, the devil wished to make one of his favourite excursions over hill and dale through Cornwall. Finding the mouth of the pit entirely closed by a huge stone, he carried it off in his hand, and began playing with it like a pebble across country. *En route*, however, he met the archangel Michael, the patron of Helston; a combat ensued between the two adversaries, and the devil, after he had been beaten in the fight, let the stone fall, thus laying the foundation of the town.

I saw the identical stone at the Angel Hotel in Helston, and affirm that it is quite black enough to come from the infernal regions. The devil, by the way, is the hero of more than adventure in the popular mythology of Cornwall; traces of him are found in most of the names given to the abysses and caverns of the county. If his visits to the interior of the county are at the present day much less frequent than formerly, he is restrained, so it is said, by the very legitimate fear of being eaten. The Cornish people are so greedy for pastry that they would catch him and put him in a pie. I may also remark here that in England the feeling for the marvellous is modified by the geological conditions of the provinces. In low and marshy regions, the mysterious personage who plays the chief part in the legends is the Will-o'-the-wisp; in mountainous countries, like Wales, where the mist assumes aërial and transparent forms round savage gorges, Fairies reign; in Cornwall, the country of mines, precipices, and rocks, the devil and the giants are supposed to have had a hand in these gloomy prodigies.

Referring to the intervention of supernatural beings the phenomena which we now attribute to natural forces, is a fact belonging to the childhood of races; but it must be allowed that in

Cornwall the character of these good or bad spirits has been fortunately appropriated by landscape features. One of the most malevolent of these fabulous beings was a certain Tregeagle, about whom all sorts of stories are told in Cornwall. This Tregeagle, so says the chronicle, was the intendant or steward of a castle, where he was the tyrant of the poor. Having one day received a sum of money from a tenant, he died before he had entered it in his account-book. Tregeagle's successor claimed the amount of the debt; the tenant refused to pay twice over, and a lawsuit ensued. In court, the supposed debtor produced a most unexpected witness; it was the ghost of Tregeagle, whom he had succeeded in evoking. The suit, as may be supposed, was at once stopped; but the difficulty now was to get rid of the spirit of the wicked man, which remained in court. The defendant was called on to remove him; but he replied that those who had rendered the apparition necessary must get rid of it as best they could. After mature deliberation, the judges condemned Tregeagle to carry from one bay to another on the coast the sand which the sea always carried back to the same spot. While Tregeagle was employed upon this Sisyphœan task, he accidentally let a sack of sand fall at the mouth of the stream. Thus were formed the bar and Looe Pool, which extend between Helston and the sea.

The town of Helston, not satisfied with having its legend, preserves an old custom whose origin has been referred by antiquarians either to the feasts of Flora, to a victory over the Saxons, or even an old Celtic observance. On the 8th of May in each year all the shops in the town are closed, as if it were a Sunday. About seven A.M. parties of children, who went into the country at daybreak, return loaded with branches; they announce in song that "the winter is past, and that they have been to the merry green wood to find summer at home." At one in the afternoon, men and women, in summer clothes and all covered with flowers, assemble in front of the town hall. Preceded by a band of musicians, they perform a very peculiar dance called the "Furry." These choregraphic evolutions at first take place in the street; but, carried away by their Bacchanalian ardour, the dancers of both sexes enter private houses, and dance in the gardens. The holiday lasts till nightfall, and terminates with a grand ball at the Angel Hotel. I am bound to add that "Furry day" is annually losing some of its old importance, and this should be regretted, for it seemed to bring together the different classes of English society. The air which the minstrels still play at the head of the procession, and which is known by the name of the "Furry tune," certainly confirms the opinion of those who regard such rites as relics of antiquity. This old air is traditional in Wales, and also, it is said, in Brittany.

From Helston to Cape Lizard, the road is monotonous and ill supplied with carriages. In spite of the introduction, still very recent, of railways, the means of communication in Cornwall still remain, in some respects, in the state of childhood. Formerly people travelled in vehicles called vans; some still exist on the old system, and the shape of these heavy vehicles has something singularly primitive about it. They consist of a huge long box, placed on wheels and entirely open at both ends. An old foundered horse drags along these vans, which are loaded with baggage, and they would never reach their destination save for a very simple circumstance. The road is either up hill or down (there are no level roads in Cornwall): when going down hill, the van presses on the horse's legs and compels it to go; up hill, the driver honestly requests the travellers to get down and push the van themselves. The omnibus which conveyed me to Cape Lizard was on a far more modern system, I confess. The driver—a true type of a Cornish peasant, with broad shoulders and a slightly bent back—was a small farmer in the neighbourhood of the cape. He urged on his horses with his voice, calling them both by name and giving them every sort of encouragement to get on. According to him, there was nothing like appealing to the feeling of animals, which did not prevent him, I must say, from giving them a hearty lash now and then.

Contrary to the general character of Cornwall, this road is flat and smooth, and bordered on each side by heaths, a few fields, and poor orchards with apple-trees half killed by moss. As I was seated on the box by the driver, I could see for an immense distance, but I had nothing around me but solitude; we only saw at rare intervals a flock of ducks sporting in a pond hidden under the grass, or some wild-looking donkeys, with bristling coats, that were devouring the thistles. About half-way to the Lizard, the shades of a great park, a species of oasis in the desert, cut for a moment the monotonous lines of the landscape. On leaving this park, I was surprised to notice, at the foot of the hedges bordering the road, patches of white heath (*erica vagans*) for the first time: we had entered the region of serpentine. The natural sympathy that exists between this plant and this rock is a fact well known to botanists; one never appears without the other. All at once this ordinary perspective of uncultivated and open commons, which had followed us from Helston, assumed a grand appearance as if by magic; at all points of the horizon the immense lines of the sea undulated before us. I was then enabled to explain the name given to this cape; it really resembles the flat head of a lizard thrusting its pointed snout into the waves.

Lizard village is composed of a few cottages, scattered over the surface of a poor and ungrateful soil. The inhabitants, especially the women, present a very peculiar type. You have scarce crossed the border of Devon and entered Cornwall, ere you are struck by a change in the human physiognomy. On the roads, in the inns, in the waggons, you continually notice oval faces with elongated features, black hair, grey eyes, prominent noses, large mouths,—in a word, the Celtic type. Are we still in England? We might doubt the fact, as we no longer see around us the round heads of the Anglo-Saxons, with the plump cheeks and light hair and whiskers. This change in the external traits evidently marks the passage from one race to another; and yet the language, trade, and manners of the population all have a thoroughly English stamp.

The Celtic family is present in the United Kingdom in three very distinct states, which betray it more or less from English society. First we have Ireland, which certainly belongs to England, but offers it a sullen opposition through religious prejudices. Next comes the principality of Wales, which, while unreservedly adopting the religion and laws of the kingdom, has still preserved its language. As for Cornwall, it has not only been for a long time subject to and incorporated with the English nation, but it has also entirely lost its old idiom. History, which has frequently devoted touching pages to wars which have forcibly annexed provinces within a state, has paid but slight notice to the slow and gradual infiltration of the influences which really complete the conquest. Language being to nations what style is to individuals, the extinction of an idiom is far from being an insignificant fact—it is the sign of an ancient nationality abdicating.

The primitive language of Cornwall was a Celtic dialect. The inhabitants of this province assert that they were civilized before the rest of Great Britain, and base the assertion on various historic records. Diodorus Siculus says that "the natives of this part of Britain were not only very hospitable, but also highly cultivated in their manners, owing to their relations with foreign merchants." He here doubtless alludes to the metal trade, which attracted to the coast the ships of the Phœnicians, and perhaps of the Greeks. The learned men of Cornwall, moreover, assert that their language had a wealth and softness of pronunciation which could not be found to the same degree in Wales or Brittany. This language was spoken in Cornwall nearly to the close of the 17th century. Daily menaced by the invasions of English, it appears to have retreated and maintained itself for a longer period on the coasts. The rector of Landeweduack, near the Lizard, was, Borlase tells us, the last who still preached in Celtic shortly before 1687.

Is the primitive language of Cornwall an utterly extinct idiom at the present day? Yes and no. It is no longer spoken, but a vocabulary is preserved in the Cottonian Library, and other MSS. survive it. The names it gave to localities, more especially to rocks and promontories, have remained vigorously attached to these immovable monuments of nature. On the other hand, some of the Celtic words have returned under ground again; they are found at the bottom of the mines in the familiar language of the workmen. Proverbs and other relics of this venerable language also wander about the modern idiom of the inhabitants, to which they impart a sententious character. I will only quote two of these maxims: "In summer remember winter;" "Expect nothing good from a long tongue; but a man without a tongue will lose his land."

The Celtic race extends over the whole of Cornwall; but it was from Falmouth to Cape Lizard that it appeared to me to offer the purest type, especially among women. In the latter locality, tradition has it that there was formerly an infusion of Spanish blood. This hypothesis is supported by certain Castilian names which have been preserved among the villagers, and by the physical traits of the inhabitants. It is perfectly true that you find among them here and there traces of a southern origin,—for instance, an olive complexion and a rich profusion of black hair. This is certainly, in the absence of documents supported by history, a very fragile base on which to erect an ethnological theory. Such characteristics might have been produced by the climate; for even at the Lizard wild plants are found which grow nowhere else in England, and which essentially belong to hot countries.

Imagination, however, has gone still farther; the English have lately tried to enlighten through proper names certain questions that have remained obscure in the study of human races. The tendency is certainly excellent, but still it must not be abused. Miss Yonge, who recently published a very curious book on the "History of Christian names," fancies she has found in Cornwall traces of the commerce of the old inhabitants with Phœnicia; and these traces are the names of Amubal and Zenobia, which are very frequent in the country. More than one objection might be raised to this Utopia, and yet accident made me acquainted with an old fisherman who entirely shared the same views. As age had deprived him of his strength, he generally confided to his eldest son the duty of casting the nets.

The first time I met this man was near the Lion's Den: seated on a rock, he was gazing at the sea, which was calm at that moment, but agitated even in its repose, like the conscience of the just man. His wife, who was nearly as old as himself, declared that he was only fit to tell stories. It was to hear some of these that I went several times to his house. This was a cottage strangely built, half of magnificent serpentine stones, half of yellow mud dried in the sun, and covered with a thatch. The stone wall supported that part of the house most exposed to the sea winds, while the gables and front were made of clay. A good brushwood fire crackled in the chimney to boil the kettle, and it was by the side of this fire that the worthy fisherman recounted to me the origin of the inhabitants of the coast. It was an authentic fact, he added, and the proof was that he had heard it told to his grandfather.

A queen of the name of Zenobia undertook a long sea voyage in order to see with her own eyes that famous Cornish coast, which had been represented to her as so rich in metals. Did she come from Tyre or Sidon? This question the good fisherman could not precisely answer; it was so long ago! However this may be, the sea which bathes the West of England was as wicked and stormy then as it is now. The vessel, on board of which was the queen, was wrecked on the rocks. About this latter point the fisherman was much more positive; he could point me out the very spot, he said. All the courtiers who accompanied Zenobia were drowned, while the sailors, who were good swimmers, succeeded in reaching the coast. While saving themselves, they were careful to save the queen and two or three of her maids of honour. Cast on a desert and unknown beach, they did not omit preparing a shelter for the night under which their sovereign could worthily rest. A large sail was drawn out of the sea, dried, and formed into a tent. The sailors laid their garments on the ground, cut large branches in the forests that existed at that day, and formed a roof of foliage over the queen's bed. At nighttime the queen, doubtless touched by the respect and devotion of these poor subjects, who only thought of her in their disasters, granted them the honour of kissing her hand. The rough sailors, kneeling down, performed in turn a ceremony which they had seen carried out with greater grace by the lords on board the vessel. A boy of twelve years of age was chosen as page; and with a bough in his hand fanned the august face of Zenobia, doubtless in memory of an Oriental country where there were mosquitoes and the heat was stifling. The queen, exhausted with fatigue, slept soundly, just as soundly as if she had been lying on a purple couch.

The next morning the shipwrecked men spread along the coast, but could only see the relics of their ship, and waves roaring behind other waves. They had neither tools nor the necessary means for building other vessels. For whole days they gazed intently on the sea, seeking to discover some sail in the distance; at the expiration of a certain time, seeing nothing come, they lost all hope of returning to their country, and began constructing cabins. They erected one for the queen; this hut, built of earth and wood, was not equal to her old palace; but still she must be contented with it. They offered her consolation by bringing her fine lumps of tin, rare stones, and crystals. As the small stock of provision they had managed to save from the wreck soon became exhausted, they were obliged to think about obtaining a livelihood. Some of the old sailors started in pursuit of wild beasts: the majority, however, cut down trees and dug out canoes with which to fish. The queen saw her people disperse with sorrow; and the very zeal of her ex-subjects soon began to grow cold amid the hard labours imposed by necessity. Her rich gold and silk robes fell to pieces, and she was only too glad to substitute seal-skins for them. Her maids of honour, despairing about marrying princes, consented, after some hesitation, to ally themselves with poor sailors. At the commencement they willingly left their huts once or twice a day to give a helping hand in the queen's household; but with years children came, and their time was fully occupied with their own family. Zenobia's page himself grew tired of fanning the queen, and exchanged the branch for an oar.

The queen complained bitterly; but seeing that her complaints were of no use, and that all hands were occupied elsewhere, she bravely resolved to serve herself. As she was still young she grew tired of widowhood, and became a fisherman's wife. While the latter was at sea, she cultivated a few vegetables round the hut, made the soup, and on her husband's return spread his wet clothes before the fire. As they loved each other, they were happy and had plenty of children. These children, accustomed from their tenderest age to follow their father in the boat and cast nets, became skilful fishermen; besides they had no difficulty in forgetting their rights to a throne, and consoling themselves for the loss of a grandeur they had never known. It is, however, from this blood royal, if we may believe the simple chronicler, that the principal fishermen's families scattered along the Cornish coast are descended.

In spite of these efforts of imagination and legend to fasten on by a few links to a Phœnician origin, it is very certain that the inhabitants of Cornwall, taken in a mass, are simply ancient Britons who have become English. They have been compared to the Scotch and the natives of Wales, with whom they certainly possess a family likeness; but Lizard village reminds the visitor very much of Ireland. The shape of the cabins is nearly the same, and, to complete the resemblance, pigs wander about the streets with an air of majestic satisfaction. Some traces of Irish humour are also met with now and then among the lower classes of the population.* Clever and insinuating, these western Britons have fortunately associated the traits of the Celtic character with the strength of will that distinguishes the Anglo-Saxon type.

The fishermen at the Lizard are scattered about the village; but their gathering-place is a bay known by the name of Lizard Fishery Cove. This deep and retired bay opens between two walls of cliffs that shelter it from the winds. A clear stream, forming cascades, descends by a stone staircase which it has itself dug along the rough flanks of the rock. The top of a small hill, round which a hollow way winds, is occupied by a few fishermen's cottages gaily adorned with fuchsias and geraniums; but the road suddenly sinks and runs through sand to the sea. In a corner stands a small building without doors or windows, under which is a capstan to pull the boats out of the water when it is found necessary to beach them. Further on is another clumsy building, half stone, half mud, surmounted by an angular roof supported by rough granite pillars; it is the fish

---

* It is very difficult to analyze these *nuances*; the best plan will be to supply a specimen. A Cornish peasant was summoned as witness against a boy charged with a slight offence. The magistrate asked the peasant if the boy usually spoke the truth. "Yes," the other replied; "he speaks the truth, and sometimes a little more than the truth." This is what the English call an Irishism.

cellars, in which fish are kept and salted. The entrance of this miniature port is guarded seawards by enormous rocks running out into the water and forming a species of quay.

At the time when I visited the cove, that is to say about midday, the fishermen's wives, standing or seated on the rocks beaten by the waves, were waiting till their husbands could come in. As the tide was high and the breeze strong, the boats had a great difficulty in reaching this beach, which was studded with shoals. As soon as one of the boats was able to overcome the obstacle, the women held out to the fishermen a basket in which was their dinner. The latter then put out to sea again, and after enjoying their modest meal continued to cast their nets. It was, as the women themselves said, a grand sight; four fishing boats, assisted by six other smaller boats, which with their oars resembled sea-spiders, were tossing on the huge blue waves. The men threw out their interminable nets, forming circles on the sea; and then at intervals they passed from one boat to the other a bottle full of restorative liquor.

The Lizard fishermen have a sturdy struggle against the grandeurs and dangers of a formidable coast. The coast is to a certain extent serrated with upright promontories, between which are horseshoe creeks hollowed out in the solid mass of the rocks. For the artist who only seeks the splendours of nature, this configuration is admirable. Kynance Cove, for instance, defies comparison with all the other Cornish bays. Imagine a group of headlands broken by precipices and rising in face of rocks which have fallen into the sea. The fishermen, not knowing how to explain this pile of ruins, say that the fiend one day had the idea of building a hedge for the smugglers between France and England; but, as frequently happens in Cornwall, his projects were foiled by the army of celestial spirits, and, being pursued, he let all the rocks fall at the entrance of Kynance Cove. Some of the rocks only rise to the surface of the sea, and their place is thus marked by a circle of foam; others, on the contrary, rise boldly and with singular outlines above the angry waves, which cover them a few moments with a fringe of snow, and then fall back in a cascade on the black and polished base of these monoliths. Some, erect as columns, regard the waves with an air of defiance, and seem to say to them: " You shall not rise to me." Of all the marvels of this savage-looking coast, those which struck me most are the caverns.

These caverns, some of which run into frightful and perpendicular precipices, have received peculiar names, such as Pigeon's Hugo, Raven's Hugo, and the Devil's Frying-pan. The last is situated near Cadgwith, a small fishing village sheltered by steep hills, possessing what the

English call a romantic character. Here I hired a boat; the sea was perfectly calm, and no boatman of Cadgwith would venture near this dangerous coast in dubious weather. We first visited the Frying-pan, which, seen from the coast, certainly offers grand features; in the dark mass of rocks opens an arch, into which the light of day pours, and under which aquatic birds fly.

We continued our excursion by water to Dolor Hugo, whose real name is Dollah Hugo: that of Dolor, which has prevailed in the familiar language, is probably derived from the stern melancholy imprinted on the general appearance of this den, into which the waves rush day and night like wild beasts. The entrance is formed by rocks of a magnificent colour, whose arch rises to an imposing height. This entrance is at first wide enough for a six-oared boat to pass; but it soon narrows, and the end is lost in darkness. As far as the eye can penetrate, the water rises and falls with a mournful plash against the rocks. I was beginning to feel lost in the mystery and solemnity of this scene, when I was suddenly startled by a formidable explosion. If a thunder-bolt had fallen through the roof it could not have produced a more fearful sound, and it rebounded, as it were, from pillar to pillar, as if reflected by all the echoes of the cavern. Through a cloud of settling smoke, I saw the smiling and malicious face of my boatman, a young fisherman of Cadgwith, who, without warning me, had amused himself with firing a pistol. He wished to frighten me; the tourist surprised by this terrible commotion in fact believes that the whole line of cliffs has been shaken by an earthquake, and is about to fall in ruins. My guide, however, refused to go further, and indeed the boat was almost squeezed by the two walls of rock. I asked him if any one had ever explored the depths of the cavern. To do so, he replied, a clever and intrepid swimmer would be required. The fishermen of Cadgwith are brave, but they do not like to incur useless danger, and not one of them has as yet penetrated more than a few yards into this sinister mouth.

The rocks that form the natural ramparts of the Lizard are of a very various nature; they are composed of granite, talc, micaceous slate, but above all, of serpentine. This name comes from the resemblance which was supposed to be found between the colours of this stone and those of a serpent's skin. Nothing in fact can equal the beauty of this rock, spotted with black, white, green, yellow, and red, and polished by the continual action of the sea. It has only one fault at this spot, that of being too common. The districts invaded by this stone lose the roads bordered by quickset hedges, which are one of the charms of an English landscape; for these fresh and shady tracks are substituted by the

Lizard walls, on which people walk and which serve as roads. Walking upon walls does not appear at the first blush a very agreeable exercise. As, however, these roads made by human hands are sufficiently wide and always dry, you walk along them readily enough. Serpentine is not exclusively employed in constructing roads or houses; the finest specimens are carefully gathered and employed in the arts.

One day, when I had lost myself on the downs that surmount the cliffs, I was suddenly surprised by a storm. The thunder rolled over the sea, preceded by flashes of lightning which inflamed the surface of the waves. I sought a place of shelter, but, as far as I could see, there was no sign of a habitation; I only saw some frightened sheep trying to shelter themselves beneath the monstrous blocks of stone piled up at regular intervals on the top of the precipices. Wet through, I followed hap-hazard a path that ran down a deep gorge, when to my great satisfaction I discovered on the sea-shore, and on the other side of a torrent that dashed over the rocks, a boy about a dozen years of age. He made me signals to point out the direction I should follow. By my guide's advice I crossed, by a natural bridge of tottering stones, the torrent already swollen by the rains, and found myself in a narrow valley, or, more correctly speaking, in a nook of ground closed on both sides by large hills. The boy walked bravely before me, and led me to a humble cottage, picturesquely situated on a rock, with a large mill-wheel at its side. Here I sat down by the fire by invitation of the mistress of the house, who was the mother of several little children collected round her like a covey. Her husband's trade was polishing curious stones and cutting out of serpentine inkstands, vases, lamps, and all sorts of artistic objects, which his wife sold to visitors. In the village there are several of these shops of local curiosities. Two wealthy companies, Penzance Serpentine Company and Lizard Serpentine Company, have also been established for some years to work this stone on a large scale and by means of powerful machinery. At the present day columns, chimney-pieces, and other architectural ornaments, are made of it.

Stone-cutting, agriculture, and fishing supply the inhabitants of the Lizard with a livelihood. The fishing is rather abundant, and embraces a rich variety of fish. Turbot is caught on this coast, but I learned with amazement that the Cornish fishermen do not care much for it: they frequently cut it in pieces to tempt the greed of the lobster, that Lucullus of the sea. The reason for this sacrifice is that the fishermen can easily keep the lobsters alive, and thus wait for the orders of the London fishmongers, while they have great difficulty in keeping turbot. Of all the fish that repay the Cornish fishery, only one, however, deserves to fix our attention as being peculiar to the west coast, and this fish is the pilchard. The pilchard visits the coast of the Lizard, and 6,500 barrels, each containing 2,400 or 2,500 of these fish, were exported to Italy in 1862.

At the Land's End the granitic masses suddenly attain a Cyclopean and formidable development. The rocks that stud this promontory form the last vertebræ of the great back-bone of England. A chain of hills commencing in Cumberland forms toward the north a first group of haughty and savage peaks, only interrupted by the lowlands of Lancashire and Cheshire, and the cliffs of the Bristol Channel. The second group, called the Cambrian system, gradually descends as it runs from the north to the south of Wales. A third system of hills, not nearly so high, the Devonian, separated from the Cambrian by the Bristol Channel, runs through Gloucestershire, Wiltshire, Somerset, and Devon, and expires at the Land's End.

The visitor, however, must not expect to find here a proud promontory, piling rock on rock, like the Cape of Cornwall. The ground, on the contrary, descends as if it wished to fall humbly into the sea; all at once, however, it rises, defended as it is by a double or triple line of cliffs which offer a battle front to the waves. These bones of the globe, which suddenly lacerate the terrestrial crust, have an austere character; you stand respectfully before the venerable masses of granite, the first-born of things on the surface of our planet.

The visitor reaches the promontory of the Land's End, the Belerium of the Romans, by following a path, by the side of which stand grey rocks resembling ancient tombs. The promontory itself, or headland, is composed of a series of rocks which advance into the sea like the bastions of a fortress. At the end of these natural ramparts, you notice the wide waves of the Atlantic beating the wall of granite with the sombre and monotonous noise of an eternity. The restless waves and motionless rocks admirably represent the contrast between movement and resistance. On seeing this army of waves rushing with blind fury against the reef, and beating a retreat after having been broken and divided, you would be inclined to say that the wave is conquered. But that would be an error. The rock wears out and the wave does not. The defeat is slow, I confess, for the granite assumes even on the surface of the repulsed waters an air of empire and triumph; but look at the base, it is undermined. The sea hollows in these solid masses mysterious passages, perfidious anpactriosities into which the contracted and troubled water bursts with a dull roar; it gnaws but little, but it constantly gnaws. These ravages heighten the solemnity of the scene.

Land's End is one of the most imposing sites

to be found on the coasts of England. Here, on a stone which is still shown to visitors, pious John Wesley wrote a hymn; here too, Turner, the painter of desolate horizons, celebrated God in another form by drawing these lines of water, earth, and rocks. The spectacle is, in fact, religious and sublime. Far as the eye can see, it only perceives the gloomy desert of the upheaved waves, above which floats the dispersed fleece of clouds. A grey sky is needed for these fugitive perspectives of the sea, for this affecting monotony of melancholy. And yet the name of Land's End is a geographical falsehood; beyond that ending point of land, another land begins—you have America before you. To this new world, veiled by distance, and, as it were, drowned on the horizon by all the waters of the abyss, I sent my humble voice: may American society emerge from the civil wars, glorious and delivered from the shadows of slavery, like the sun which shines at intervals on the Atlantic!

The Land's End is not the only marvel to be found at the extremity of Cornwall; the whole coast abounds with bold promontories, among which I will especially mention Pardenick. It is composed of rectangular blocks of granite, laid one upon the other so as to form columns. The English greatly admire this natural arrangement of the rocks, and in truth, what architecture is superior to this? In the piled-up relics which face the sea, the eye discovers arches, arcades, pillars, almost as perfect as if they had been carved with the chisel; in a word, all the types of historic edifices.* Imagination goes further still; it fancies it can trace resemblances between the shapes of these rocks and certain human faces; it is thus that the popular language of Cornwall has given the name of "Dr. Johnson" to a round and massive stone, and that of "Dr. Syntax" to a granite rock which fairly represents the head of an old schoolmaster. Sculpture, perhaps, had no other origin; the first men, struck by fortuitous resemblances which existed between certain blocks of natural rock and the living beings thus had before them, may have conceived the idea of statues. Other masses of granite fallen into the sea have also received curious names round the Land's End; here is the Knight, with his armour and plumes of stone; here too is the Irish Lady. To this latter stone, if tradition may be believed, an Irish girl tried to cling with her nails after a shipwreck in which all the passengers aboard the

* In order to properly appreciate the beauties of this coast, it is necessary frequently to descend to the base of the rocks by steep paths bordered by precipices. An Englishman, who was at the Land's End at the same time as myself, had made a peculiar study of this art; he knew infallibly the stone on which the foot must be placed to escape a roll in the sea. His enthusiasm excited him voluntarily to perform the duties of a guide. All the reward he derived for his services—and he considered it enough—was to be able to say, "I led Lord and Lady ——— to the foot of Carn-Cowall (one of the most abrupt rocks in the vicinity of Land's End); they would never have got there without me."

same vessel had perished. It was, however, a vain effort, the waves carried her away, and she now walks on moonlit nights upon the trembling waves with a white rose between her lips. Several fishermen have seen her, and bluntly bear evidence to the truth of the fact.

Near the Land's End, and still nearer the Irish Lady, stands on the coast, in a series of terraces, the little village of Senum, exclusively inhabited by fishermen. It consists of a group of houses clumsily cut in the granite; the stones of these huts have hardly been found by water. However poor it may be, the fisherman's house is to him what the nest is to the sea-bird. Built on the side of a rock or in the hollow of a bay sheltered from the winds, it represents to him repose after a tempest. Hence I resolved to enter one of these abodes covered with thatch and with narrow windows, which form here the type of domestic architecture. A bill announcing a small retail trade furnished me with an opportunity for entering without appearing indiscreet. I was agreeably surprised; the interior of the house was much better than the exterior. A chimney with a bunk, inside which blazed a coal fire; a ceiling painted blue, along which fish were drying on a sort of hurdle; a sanded floor, a dresser covered with china and glass: everything in this cottage breathed comfort and cleanliness. A humble chandler's shop was kept in the back room.

This fishing village belongs entirely, with its houses, boats, and nets, to a single proprietor—a man without children the woman who gave me these details added, as she looked proudly at her small family. Some few inhabitants of Senum, however, possess small boats, and are thus enabled to fish with a line on their own account. Boys of ten years of age prepare the hooks, and in a small boat riding on the storm, they catch large fish, which they carry with delight to their mothers. In vain do the parents dream at times of some other trade but the fisherman's for these boys: the sea attracts them, I was told, as the river attracts ducklings. Some of them, however, receive a certain amount of education. As I was walking along the scarped flanks of the village, the sea suddenly assumed an alarming appearance. The sun disappeared, a black dense fog settled down like a veil on the surface of the sea, and entirely concealed two rocks which, under the name of the Sisters, form one of the striking features of the horizon. It was the precursive sign of a storm. I took refuge under the porch of an old granite house, in which a school was kept. Invited to enter, I found a room with bare and dilapidated walls, and boys and girls sitting on benches on both sides. The schoolmistress complained bitterly of the locality, as too hot in summer, too cold in winter, and at all times uninhabitable. The poverty of this school harmonizes well with the sad stern air of the village. Some of the children write and read passably; they would make greater progress if they attended more assiduously; but, as soon as the potato harvest or the fishing season arrives, they fly off, some into the fields, others upon the sea, which is then covered with sails. The boys become in a short time skilful sailors, and they must be so, for the coasts bristle with reefs and are visited by terrible squalls. When the wind blows at the Land's End, it blows heavily; and "A man," say the inhabitants of Senum, "then wants two other men to hold his hair on his head."

Such hurricanes necessarily produce many catastrophes. Most affecting stories are told at Senum. Some years ago, a ship was driven by the wind into a cave in the side of a rock; the whole crew perished with the exception of four men. Among the dead, two sailors were found in each other's arms: they were two friends who had passed through a thousand dangers together; they had been prisoners of war in France under the first Empire; and together, too, they had lived to escape from shipwreck. They were buried under the turf at the foot of the cliff, without being parted, in the same position as they were found.

On June 12th, 1851, another ship was dashed against the Sisters, and the passengers sought a refuge on the two isolated rocks in the middle of the waves. The sea was so furious that no one could approach them, and they were washed off one after the other by the waves, with the exception of Captain Saunderson and his wife, who remained for two days in sight of a trembling population incapable of assisting them. At length the brave fishermen, at a great risk of their lives, got close enough to the rocks with their boats to throw a rope to the couple. At this moment a sublime combat began between husband and wife, each refusing to escape before the other. The wife's devotion gained the victory; she compelled Saunderson to fasten on the line, and he was immediately dragged through the waves by the fishermen, who picked him up safe and sound. It was now the wife's turn; but whether she tied the line improperly round her waist, or for some other reason, she was drowned before she reached the boat. Her tomb is now in the cemetery, with an inscription stating that she was thirty-four years of age and was a native of Newcastle-on-Tyne.

The storms, it may be supposed, do not spare the fishermen themselves on these coasts, which have been rendered illustrious by so many disasters. The master of a small public-house, 'The Ship,' now an old man, but formerly a bold fisherman, saw his father and brother, as well as his wife's father and brother, all perish together in the same boat in a squall. After this it is not surprising to find on the faces of the inhabitants of Senum a sort of melancholy gravity. The women, more especially, have a stern, sad air, features hard as the rock, and foreheads prematurely wrinkled. It is, though, a curious and animated sight to see a fleet of sixty boats putting off from Senum with their brown sails, to try the night fishing.

This village, which is much too greatly neglected by visitors, must not be confounded with another bearing the same name, further from the coast, on a hill. There is a great difference between the two, which is shewn both in the shape of the houses and the character of the inhabitants. The Senum situated inland is the gathering-place of travellers and strangers. Here is an old inn, called, owing to its eccentric position, 'The First and Last Inn in England.' Here, too, lies, near a humble shed where the village blacksmith joyously beats his iron, an enormous block of granite in the shape of a table, upon which tradition declares that three kings dined one day. One was the king of the sea, who supplied a fish caught in his empire; the second ruled over a country of forests, who sent a wild boar; the third had states which extended beneath the sun, who supplied fruits and wine. For a long time past a jealousy had existed between these sovereigns, and they had often discussed the points as to who was the greatest of the three. At the first course the lords declared that it was the lord of the seas, for the fish was delicate; at the second the king of the forests had the advantage; but at the dessert the king of the grapes gained all votes, for his wines were exquisite. As good fare and good wine dispose even rivals to be generous, the three kings agreed at the end of the banquet, that instead of disputing about the merits of one country to the detriment of another, it was better to unite them all by an interchange of their produce.

CHAPTER V.

MOUNT'S BAY—CHANGES ON THE COAST—NEWLYN AND MOUSEHOLE—APPEARANCE OF THESE TWO VILLAGES—THE PILCHARD, WHERE DOES IT COME FROM?—ITS MIGRATIONS—THE DRIFT-NET AND THE SEINE—THE FISHING FLEET—METHOD OF SPREADING THE NETS—GENERAL RESULTS OF DRIFT-NET FISHING—THE MARKET—THE QUEEN OF THE FISHWOMEN—THE CURING—THE FISH CELLAR—CAPRICES OF THE PILCHARD—A FISHERMAN'S HOME—A VOYAGE TO AUSTRALIA—DOLLY PENTREATH—SUNDAY IN A FISHING VILLAGE—JOHN WESLEY—THE DISSENTERS AND THE CHURCH OF ENGLAND—SAINT IVES—A LOST CHURCH—MR. BOLITHO'S CELLARS—SEINE FISHING—THE HUERS—THE FLOATING PRISON—PRODUCE OF THE FISHERY—MORAL CHARACTER OF THE FISHERMEN.

THE mass of granite that forms the Land's End extends on one side toward the Cape of Cornwall, near which it disappears under a stratum of slate stone, and on the other it advances toward Mount's Bay, after raising in face of the sea audacious promontories, excavating abysses in the shape of a funnel, and leaving on its track grottoes with narrow Gothic windows, through which a glimpse of the sky and of the heaving ocean may be caught. Mount's Bay (so called from its neighbour, St. Michael's Mount) opens in front of the town of Penzance. This mass of water is surrounded by coasts which have a peculiar interest for geologists. An old spit of land, composed of granite sand, and called Western Green, now only forms on the skirts of the bay an insignificant and barren shore; yet in the reign of Charles II. there were here thirty-six acres of pasture land, which have been washed away by the waves in the course of two or three centuries. Tradition also asserts that St. Michael's Mount, now an isolated rock in the sea, was formerly situated in a wood which extended several miles from the sea.* Between this mount and the village of Newlyn, which stands on the other side of the bay, there is found beneath the sand a black layer of vegetable earth full of nuts, branches, leaves, trunks, and roots belonging to trees which still grow on English soil. Such facts proclaim that there has been a change in the relative level of the land and sea, and that this change does not date back beyond an epoch when the same plants grew in Cornwall as are found there now. Other peculiarities here seem to indicate very clearly that such a revolution has taken place since the country has been inhabited by man.†

* The Celtic name confirms the tradition, for it means "the rock of the forest."

† I saw in the Penzance Museum, belonging to the Geological Society of Cornwall, a human skull, found at Senum, near the Land's End, in what is believed to be a submarine forest. This

Newlyn and Mousehole, the two fishing villages, stand on the right bank of the bay. You go there from Penzance by a road in the shape of a terrace, leaning on one side against the rocky base of the hills, and open on the other to the blue waters, which are here and there slightly tinged by sand or certain atmospheric influences. Newlyn announces itself by an old stone bridge thrown over a small stream in which ducks swim. The entrance of the village has been more than once inundated by the waters of the bay during heavy storms. Situated on a creek, it has the shape of a crescent or string bow, while the group of houses is commanded in the rear by lofty hills, with steep and abrupt sides. The view enjoyed from the quay is admirable: on one side is the town of Penzance, with its group of masts, its houses, and its granite church, which seem to float on the surface of the waves; in front rises St. Michael's Mount, crowned by its old castle rooted in the rock; further on seaward advances one of the horns of the bay formed by Cape Lizard. In the port, a

---

skull has a very curious shape, and appears to belong to the most savage type. All this coast bears the traces of old ravages, which have been attributed to an inundation produced by the sinking of the ground. As to the period of the catastrophe it is very difficult to fix. The author or authors of the *Saxon Chronicle* certainly speak of an irruption of the sea, said to have occurred in 1099; but this event, or these series of events, must go back to a much older period.

fishing flotilla, composed of about 120 smacks and other small boats, seems to be sleeping.

Mousehole, which succeeds Newlyn on the same coast, is about two miles distant from it. The road, which continues to coast and command the sea, runs between two hedges of furze and blackberry. Mousehole forms an amphitheatre in a hollow valley excavated by the sea, but which at once rises again in a circle of verdant hills, here and there rent by rocks. Facing the quay there is in the bay an islet known as St. Clement's Island, whose base offers a surface of smooth stone half submerged in the sea, while its top, visited by clouds of gulls, is covered with a short fine grass. This natural breakwater protects the mouth of the port. Not contented with this insufficient defence, the fishermen have made for themselves, recently, a large and strong jetty, which cost them £1,400. Here repose in the daytime the boats at anchor. Mousehole was formerly the metropolis of the bay, and some traces of its ancient grandeur still remain. At the present day, however, it is, like Newlyn, a village whose inhabitants find their daily bread in the sea.

In the afternoon, they are only occupied in drying their nets: a fisherman, bending beneath the weight of one of these vast and heavy nets, walks along slowly, followed by another who unfolds and extends along the side of the quay

the whole length of the fabric. The bare-armed women, with a bonnet coquettishly set on the front of the head, and a light cotton dress fastened round the waist, wash their linen or fetch water in jugs from a limpid stream that falls over rocks behind the villages. Cottages, some looking toward the quay, others grouped on the hill like a flock of goats, are surrounded by walls made of rough stones, covered with vines, whose grapes promise to ripen: they generally look neat and cheerful. The name of Mousehole has been the subject of numerous commentaries.*
Near the village there is in the cliffs a cavern whose arch-shaped entrance is rather high, but which soon contracts and forms a narrow passage leading to a gallery formerly dug by the miners. Is it this cavern which has given its name to the village? However this may be, Newlyn and Mousehole belong to Mount's Bay, one of the principal scenes of the pilchard fishery.

What is the pilchard? This fish (*Chipea pilchardus*) certainly belongs to the herring family, but is detached from it by some external characteristics: it has a shorter head, a more compact body, the dorsal fin situated more forward toward the centre of gravity, while it is covered with longer scales than the common herring.

* This spot was formerly called Porthenis, or Port Enys. *Enys*, in the primitive language of Cornwall, means an isle. It was doubtless an allusion to St. Clement's Island, which is a little distance from the port.

K

It has been christened, on account of its wandering habits, the vagabond or gipsy of the seas. The period of its arrival and departure frequently varies with the years. Where does it come from? Whither does it go? The more general opinion is that these fish pass the greater part of the winter on the coast of some northern region. A Cornish naturalist, Mr. Couch, who has greatly studied the question, believes, on the contrary, that the pilchards retire during the winter to the deep water on the west of the Scilly Islands. About the middle of spring they feel a necessity to travel and change their horizon. They then rise from the depths of the ocean, and the instinct of association collects them in small bands. As the season advances, these bands form into more numerous shoals; and toward the end of July and beginning of August the pilchards form a great army, which, under the guidance of a chief, commences that extraordinary migratory movement which annually gives rise to the finest fishery in Cornwall. Pursued by the birds of prey, which describe menacing circles in the air, and by large voracious fish, they advance in close columns. This floating multitude first touches land to the east of the Cape of Cornwall, whence a detachment turns northward toward St. Ives, while the main body passes between the Scilly Isles and the Land's End, and enters the Channel, following the undulations of the coast as far as Bigbury Bay and Start Point. Their order of march is frequently modified by the currents or the state of the atmosphere. They seem all at once to have vanished, but soon return and approach the coast in imposing force—myriads of living beings urged on by myriads.

Such is the prodigious number of these fish that they change the colour of the sea: the sea boils and leaps, the fishermen say, as if it were being heated in a caldron. The passage of these submarine battalions communicates to the surface of the waves, especially at night, a phosphorescent brilliancy, which some compare to a mountain of silver, others to liquid light, just as if the moon were melted and poured into the mass of water. Sailing vessels have been impeded or arrested in their course by these banks of pilchards, extending over a surface of seven or eight square miles, and attaining a depth of two miles in the troubled sea. At such times it is said that the water is alive, for it palpitates beneath the compact mass of animated creatures that traverse it, all laden with scales and flashes.

At the time when I visited Newlyn, that is to say, the beginning of September, the fishery was in full vigour. This pilchard fishery had been bad in Mount's Bay for some years; but it began in 1863 under far more favourable auspices, and during the last week a great many fish had been taken. The fishery women pointed out to me the surface of the bay striped with red and moving bands, which, according to them, indicated the presence of schools of pilchards. This fish requires three sorts of preparation—the boats and the nets, which form the sea equipment, and the fish cellar, which is always ashore. There are in Mount's Bay about 250 smacks, of from 12 to 22 tons. Each of these boats costs, with all the accessories, nearly £450. The crew is composed of four or five men and a boy. The shape of these boats, which are painted black, and are good sailers, has nothing remarkable about it.

There are two distinct sorts of nets, corresponding to two very different styles of fishing—the drift net, and the seine. The former is preferred in heavy weather, the second in fine weather. This depends on the season, the depth of water, and the distance from the coast. As the drift is mainly used in the Mount's Bay fishery, I will describe it first. Does it respond to the idea generally formed of a net? No; especially if we compare it with the Devon trawl—that net enfolding the fish in its perfidious cavities. The drift is a long net, having at one end a line of square pieces of cork; at the other, weights of iron or lead. The cork-squares float on the surface, while the bottom of the net sinks and maintains it in a vertical position. It forms, when extended in this way, a regular wall, three quarters of a mile in length, sometimes a mile and a half, and offers an obstacle to the progress of the pilchards. This net does not catch the fish, but they catch themselves. The size of the meshes is such that the pilchard can easily introduce its head, but cannot withdraw it, as it is held by the gills, like the barbs of an arrow. Its belly, besides, being too large, and the meshes too narrow, it remains hanging in a floating wall.

It must be night time, and the net invisible, or the fish cannot be captured in this way. Fine moonlight nights, and the luminous phenomena of the sea, are, for the same reason, unfavourable to the fishery. When the water is phosphorescent the net shows, at a great depth, like a lacework of fire. In this case the pilchard is alarmed, suspects a snare, turns to the right or left, and does not continue its voyage till it has left behind it this ill-omened brilliancy. Hence it is only on dark nights that such nets are spread in the sea, when they are allowed to drift with the current.

There are few sights more interesting than that of a small fishing fleet, with its brown sails swollen by a good breeze, bounding at sunset over the quivering waves of the bay. At the beginning of summer the pilchards keep a considerable distance from land, and then they must be pursued out at sea. As the season advances, they, on the contrary, draw nearer to the coast. A Cornish proverb says, that when the wheat is lying in the furrows the fish is sporting on the rocks. The fishing boats never go more than a mile from shore; many of them even remain in the bay, whose water pulsates with living matter. On the night when I watched the preparations for this fishing the sea was calm, and, as it were, absorbed in its magnificence beneath the last beams of the sun, which was surrounded on the horizon by clouds from which emerged floods of lurid light.

The nets are methodically spread so as to intercept along the whole line the migration of the schools of pilchards. This task ended, when night descends with all its shadows, the fishermen light a fire and make their tea. The position of the boats on the surface of the waves is then indicated by the reddish light escaping from their small stoves. These lights, which rise and fall with the movement of the sea, produce a striking effect: we are glad to recognize the hand of man and his domestic manners in the gloom that covers the shifting face of the waters. While the fishing is thus going on in the face of a wind and a dark sky, the sails are either furled or entirely lowered, and the boats are hence incapable of changing their places. What would happen if a vessel were at such a moment to pass through the sea enclosed within the frail and prolonged lines of the drift? Its keel would certainly carry away the nets. To prevent this danger, a signal is employed under such circumstances. When a steamer or other vessel is coming in the direction of the nets, it is warned to keep off by the lighting of a wisp of straw. About midnight the snares set for the fish are raised. The latter are taken out of the meshes, and after they have been thrown into a boat set apart for the purpose, the nets are let down into the sea again.

The pilchards do not travel alone; they attract after them a band of brigands, such as cod, dog-fish, and large voracious fish here called pollacks. All these marauders like to attack their prey when snared, and ofttimes the fishermen have found on raising their nets many pilchards half devoured. If the opportunity is good for the prowlers of the sea, it has also been taken advantage of by the fishermen. The latter at times throw lines round the nets, and after baiting the hook with a delicate piece of pilchard, catch at the same stroke the tyrant and the victim. Courage is required to draw some of these monsters out of the water, for instance the conger, which struggles like a boa-constrictor, and, I am assured, often gives a guttural bark. One of the fishermen on the coast was seized by the throat a few years ago by one of these rude athletes, and was only able to liberate himself by cutting off its head. The drift fishing is sometimes very productive; as many as 50,000 pilchards have been caught in one night by a single driving boat. In the morning the fishermen return to shore, and if it is curious to watch the boats put out to sea, it is still more curious to see them return with the rising sun, laden with booty.

The villages of Newlyn and Mousehole, though so peaceful in the other hours of the day, are then converted into a market, where the movement, tumult, and ardour of commerce reign. A long file of trucks extends along the beach; these vehicles, to which are fastened enormous empty baskets, known here by the name of mounds, belong to the fousters or hawkers. The latter, whip in hand, perched on rocks or standing on the projecting stones of the jetty, examine with a piercing glance the contents of the boats, and yell with all the strength of their lungs, shouting the price they are willing to give for the fish, which are affected, like all other merchandize, by the law of supply and demand. The fishermen, dressed in their long sea-boots and oilskin waterproofs, are gravely occupied in arranging the nets and forming piles of fish that glisten in the sun. Women, with bent backs, loaded with a dorser called a cowel, doubtless because some resemblance was found between it and a monk's cowl, bear the enormous loads of fish from the boats to the beach. All the people push and elbow each other, with an immense quantity of talking, performed in that singing voice peculiar to Cornwall. At length the last fishing-boat has arrived; the last truck departs with the hawker, who goes away apparently satisfied with his bargain. The village then falls back into its habitual sleep, lulled by the soft and monotonous murmur of the bay.

The fisherwomen, who go afoot and are loaded with a heavy burden, are naturally met with later than the others on the road from Newlyn to Penzance. They formerly wore a picturesque costume—a large shepherd's hat of black beaver, a gaily-coloured calico jacket, a coarse flannel skirt, an apron, and buckled shoes. This dress disappeared, ten years ago, with the Queen of the Fisherwomen. Such was the name given to an old woman, who was still very active, though an octogenarian, and celebrated for her attachment to old customs. At the time of the first great Exhibition (1851) she resolved to go to London, as she had sworn not to die without having seen the Queen of England. One fine day then, she set out on foot with her creel on her back—a Newlyn fisherwoman never travels without that —and after marching 360 miles, she at length arrived in the great city. Her dress, her original manners, her honest and deliberate air, all excited attention; she was presented to the Lord Mayor. An artist asked permission to take her portrait: the fisherwoman at first refused; but when the artist added that he was himself a child of Cornwall, she said, in a quick, smart way, "I can refuse nothing to the friends of that fine country." After the death of the Queen of the Fisherwomen, the old custom was entirely abandoned: but the women of Newlyn still offer an uncommon type of vigour, courage, and activity.

A part of the pilchard crop is sold as fresh fish in Cornwall. Its flesh is oily and strong flavoured: when mixed with potatoes, and seasoned with a little salt and vinegar, it improves the ordinary fare of the country. The pilchard is rarely seen in the London market. Altogether the fish is much less known in England than the anchovy; but it is true, on the other hand, that the anchovy is less known on the banks of the Mediterranean than the pilchard. The two seas exchange their productions.

Being before all an export article, the pilchard must naturally go through a preparatory process before leaving the coasts of Great Britain. The curing is generally intrusted to women. It is an important task, and is frequently carried on day and night. The fish, on being landed, is at once conveyed on trucks, called garries, or in baskets, to the fish cellar. This cellar, generally level with the street, is a clumsy building, like a shed, covered with a roof of massive beams, supported on badly formed stone walls or rude granite pillars. The floor, a sort of mosaic formed of sea pebbles incrusted in black and

SALTING THE PILCHARDS.

glistening ovals, has been most carefully swept, and covered with a layer of coarse salt, which extends to within five or six feet of the supporting walls. On this bed of salt are laid several rows of pilchards, with their tails turned toward the walls, and following each other in such admirable order that the floor is, as they say, paved with fish. This is the foundation of the edifice, which greatly varies, according to the taste of the architect or the arrangement of the spot. Most frequently the pilchards thus piled up rise into a long and massive wall; other times they form semicircles or columns, though always with their heads turned outwards. They thus remain in bulk for four or five weeks, with a bed of salt between each layer, and subjected to a powerful pressure. The floor of the cellar slopes gently from the walls to the centre: this arrangement is essential; the oil and water daily escaping from the heap of fish thus run into a gutter, and are conveyed to the mouth of a pit, into which they flow. When the salting process is supposed to be sufficiently advanced, the pilchards are removed from the mass built with so much skill, and after being washed and cleaned they are packed in hogsheads. Each of these barrels must contain 2,400 fish. In order to reduce the bulk and extract the oil, the pilchards thus packed are pressed for another week. This final operation is effected by means of a lid, on which presses a beam, balanced at each end by two heavy balls of granite, each representing a weight of about 400 lbs. When this has been done the pilchard is ready for market.

Very few of these salt fish are consumed in England; they are sent to Naples, where they form the delight of the Lazzaroni, and to other Mediterranean ports. It is a remarkable fact that the Protestant nations of the North mainly supply the Catholic nations of the South with the means of keeping Lent, by sending them the produce of their fishery. The refuse pilchards, which could not be conscientiously put in the barrels, are sold as manure, and they are in great demand. The salt employed to cure the fish generally comes from Liverpool. It arrives at Newlyn and Mousehole in small carts painted red, drawn by an old horse and built in a very primitive manner. The women unload it into their cowels; and for the whole fishing season, only salt and fish are to be seen in the village.

Formerly, that is to say sixty or eighty years ago, the pilchard remained till Christmas off the Cornish coast: but the fish is capricious; at present the fishing begins about July, and ends toward the close of November. Afloat and ashore, this fishery supplies work in Mount's Bay to 5,000 or 6,000 persons—men, women, and children. The profits are at times very considerable. The mode of payment varies greatly, according to the private arrangements and agreements; but most frequently it is founded on the partnership between capital and labour. Of the partners, some furnish the boat, others buy the nets, while others again only bring their arms. The money for the fish sold at market is divided among all those interested, according to the value set on the share of each, either on the materials or on the fishing itself. The crew consequently are not on wages; they depend for their earnings on the fortune of the nets. Hence we find among the bay fishermen an air of ease and pride which forms a singular contrast with the sadness and humiliation of the fishermen at the Land's End. Both live almost entirely from the sea; but the first are masters, the second labourers.

At Newlyn, an old fisherman, with a worthy and respectable face, cordially offered to show me his house and dependencies. He had two cellars, one to contain his fishing instruments, and the other to salt pilchard. His house was small, but extremely clean and convenient. The sitting room, in which scarce four persons could sit, and which in this respect resembled a ship's cabin, was furnished with a species of luxury: an old clock ticked merrily in a mahogany case; an old Bible, splendidly bound and gilt, glistened on a table covered with a flowered cloth; a small glass cupboard contained rich china; and in a frame on the wall figured the genealogical table of the family. This latter circumstance sufficiently indicates a peculiar trait in the character of the peasants. They attach much importance to birth.

The boy children are also distinguished by a great spirit of enterprise and an independent character. Some years ago, some young fishermen of Newlyn resolved to go and seek their fortunes in Australia. How could they cross 3,000 miles of water without money? The difficulty was soon solved: they had among them a fishing boat of about twelve tons, which they set to work fitting up. This done, they hoisted sail and soon lost sight of the quiet houses of the hamlet, when many hearts were alarmed at their departure. Out at sea, they were obliged to trace their maritime chart out of their own heads. Half the crew slept on deck, while the other half watched, held the tiller, and consulted the stars or the compass. After considerable efforts they reached Australia. I was introduced to one of these bold navigators on the road to Newlyn, where he was walking with his wife. After remaining four years in Australia, he returned to Cornwall, where he now holds a good situation on board an ex-man-of-war.

Going to Australia or New Zealand is a sort of sport for persons born on the coast. There are very few families which have not some of their members at the antipodes. They would recoil from a journey on land; and you find many inhabitants of Newlyn or the Lizard who have never been to London or to the interior of the county: but the sea lies open before them—the sea which, as it were, roared round their cradle, and they readily intrust themselves to this old acquaintance. The women yield like the men to this seduction of space, to the dreams of fortune and happiness which float among the clouds, behind mountains of water. About seven years ago, a fisherman started for Australia in an emigrant ship, leaving in one of the bay villages a girl to whom he was engaged. Not hearing from him, and fancying herself forgotten, she collected the money for her passage, and bravely went to join him. On her arrival she learnt that the young man had lived for some time in Victoria, but had just set out again for England. The fisherman, in fact, had left Australia, with the intention of getting married; great was his disappointment when he found that his betrothed was still so far from him. Love is more powerful than the sea and distances: the fisherman worked hard, and saved up enough to get back to Australia. This time he found his betrothed, who had gone into service with a wealthy family. They now keep a small inn in the vicinity of Penzance, where I lodged for some days.

Those fishermen who have managed to escape

from the accidents of the sea generally attain a great age. The Cornish coast presents, especially as regards women, very remarkable instances of longevity. This circumstance has been attributed to the food, which usually consists of fish, to a hard and active life, but also to the mildness of the climate. At Mousehole lived Dolly Pentreath, a fisherwoman very celebrated in Cornwall, as being the last person who spoke the primitive language of the county. She died in 1778, at the age of 102, and was buried in the churchyard of St. Paul's, a pretty church which crowns the steep summit of a green hill. Outside the churchyard stands a pyramid erected by Prince Louis Lucien Bonaparte and the Rev. John Cussett, vicar of St. Paul's, in June, 1860; on this stone, sacred to the memory of Dolly Pentreath, it is stated that the Cornish dialect became extinct in this parish in the eighteenth century. In order to prove, too, that this dialect has not been entirely lost by the learned, the fifth commandment has been engraved on the granite in English and in the old language. Several objections have been raised against this monument, or at least against the fact whose memory it preserves. Languages, it is said, do not die in this way, and it is not quite certain that old Dolly Pentreath carried away with her the last sign of Briton nationality. However this may be, there is at the entrance of this same cemetery an unhewn granite stone, with a bench on either side, which preserves the memory of an old custom. On this stone the coffin was laid at burials, and the relatives or friends sat by its side as if bidding a last farewell to the defunct. It was the last halt on the road to Eternity.

Any one who wishes to form an idea of the elegance that prevails in these fishing villages, should visit Newlyn or Mousehole on a Sunday. On this day all the houses have performed their toilette: men, women, children, shine, so to speak, in white linen, silk, and lace. The observance of Sunday is one of the great religious practices in Cornwall. Near Liskeard, you are shown three enormous circles of stone called the Hurlers; and tradition declares that they are men who were metamorphosed in this way for hurling a sort of ball on the day of the Christian Sabbath. Not far from St. Just there is another circle of the same sort, known by the name of the Merry Maidens; and these girls were also changed into stones for dancing on that day. The fishermen of Mount's Bay, it must be added, were for a long time insensible to these terrible menaces; they liked to keep Sunday amid pleasures; but several years ago a great change was introduced among them by the influence of the Wesleyans or Methodists.

John Wesley played a great part in the reformation, and the traces of his passage are repeatedly found in Cornwall. I saw, close to Penzance, in the village of Hea, a small chapel in which is piously kept the rock on which Wesley preached the gospel of Christ from 1743 to 1760. At Gwennap there is a vast open air amphitheatre of an oval shape, where he also preached, and where 30,000 of his disciples assemble at the present day on Whit-Monday. At Newlyn and Mousehole there are Wesleyan chapels; and Sunday schools, attended by some two or three hundred scholars, entirely in the hands of the Methodists. In France, where discussion is not greatly permitted, it might be imagined that such force of dissenting opinions alarm and desolate the Anglican Church, and yet I affirm that it is not so; in this country of liberty, the official clergy and the sects have divided the Lord's vineyard between them. By his education, his fortune, and the style of his sermons, the Anglican minister is kept somewhat aloof from the people: the latter like simple language, and leaders who, if not very enlightened, at least share their wants and labours. They find all this in the chapels. Methodism is a narrow circle of doctrine, but it is distinctly and vigorously traced. It proposes less to instruct than to engrave on rough natures the essential features of morality. In Cornwall, the Methodist preachers like to borrow from the Bible those images of the yawning pit, and the spirit floating on the waters, which so well suit a population of miners and fishermen.

We have seen that it is the drift fishing which chiefly distinguishes Mount's Bay. The inhabitants of Newlyn and Mousehole also use the seine, which occupies about 1,000 persons, and commands a capital of £8,000 to £10,000; but the latter system of nets principally prevails at St. Ives. We must go to that town, therefore, to witness under more favourable conditions a grand fishing spectacle.

On going from Penzance to St. Ives by Hayle, you soon leave the rocks for sand. These shifting sand-banks have inundated fields which were formerly cultivated. At certain spots they have left hills and chains of downs which rise to several hundred feet above the level of the sea. On digging into this sand the ruins of old buildings have been found. A farm near St. Gwithian was attacked during the night by this dry flood, and the farmer's family were obliged to escape by the windows. In the winter of 1808, the house, which had been buried for a century, reappeared of its own accord. I saw near Hayle the old church of St. Phillack, menaced and almost overwhelmed by the yellowish masses that surround it, and which are here called towans. It seems in great peril of being swallowed up some day, like others which have disappeared in the same way; for instance, the lost church of Preranza-Buloc. Recently, however, a way has been discovered of fixing the vagabond and capricious temper of the sands by planting the *arundo arenaria*, a sort of grass or reed that grows well on downs and on the sea-shore. At other points, as at New Quay, these sands harden into stone, owing to an oxide of iron held in solution in the water that penetrates them. These stones, which to some extent may be seen visibly forming, have been considered strong enough to build houses of.

The town of St. Ives is admirably situated at the end of a bay, round which it forms a crescent, and is surrounded by sand-hills bordered by cliffs. It has been compared to a Greek village. It is quite certain that the blue sky, the green sea, the hills with their white sides, and the black rocks with their vigorous lines, compose, with the town seated in a hollow, a delicious picture. On the quay stand the old buildings of an abandoned mine: farther on, a church, protected from the sea by a stout wall, and surrounded by a cemetery, bravely offers to the waves its old stained glass windows, which have many times been beaten by the storm. Unfortunately St. Ives does not gain by being seen more closely. The more beautiful its position is, the more do its narrow, winding streets appear made to sadden visitors and dispel illusions. It is a thorough fishing town. Nearly all the houses have stone steps outside, leading to the first floors, where the families live, while the ground floors are occupied by the fish-cellars. The latter spread through the inhabited parts of the houses exhalations which are far from being agreeable, especially in the pilchard season; but the fishermen scent in this fish an odour quite as good as another—the fragrance of gain and prosperity.

The buildings intended to receive and prepare the pilchard attain considerable proportions at St. Ives. I convinced myself of this on visiting the cellars and stores of Mr. Boletho. These cellars, covered by a gallery supported by iron columns, open on a square yard, and resemble cloisters as much through their size as through the solidity of the architecture. Here you find mountains of salt brought from Spain; two pits, from which as many as 1,500 barrels of oil are drawn in good seasons. Here, when the season is advanced, pyramids of fish rise against the walls. The stores in which the nets and other apparatus are kept are also scrupulously clean, and on a vast scale. It is to the power of the capital employed in the fishing material that the English in great measure owe their success; it is mainly in this way that they acquire the riches of the sea. In the port are the masts of sixty luggers—large vessels which annually pursue the mackerel, from March to June. They then go to seek the herrings off Ireland, and return to St. Ives in the autumn, for the pilchard fishing. There are also 249 boats which, owing to the net they employ, have received the name of seine boats. The seine differs from the drift net in the meshes being smaller; but it also attacks its prey under quite other conditions. The net of Mount's Bay is a wall; the net of St. Ives is a tomb. The drift fishing takes place in the silence of dark nights; the seine fishing is performed in broad daylight, or on moonlit nights.

When I arrived at the town the whole population was in commotion; they were expecting the pilchards. This fish generally comes to St. Ives later than to Newlyn. There are even years when it does not come at all. Judge of the consternation of the inhabitants at such times! Men called huers, or hewers, were watching for its arrival, posted on hills that commanded the bay facing the town. These men have an extraordinary quick sight; they guess the movements of a school of pilchards by the colour of the sea and by the birds soaring in the sky. As such a watch demands the utmost attention, these videttes are relieved every three or six hours.

While the huers are thus watching on the top of the cliffs, three boats, manned by twenty-two men, and accompanied by smaller boats, one of which I had contrived to enter, were floating on the surface of the bay. We merely followed the movement of the waves, almost without changing our situation. The eyes of the fishermen, turned towards the spot whence the signal for action would come, were full of impatience and anxiety. We watched thus for half a day, which seemed to me very long; but my companions had been watching above a week. At length two huers appeared on the heights with "white bushes" in their hands: this is the name given to furze bushes covered with tow or white ribbons. This was the signal. The cry of "Heva! heva! heva!" then ran along from wave to wave, from rock to rock, nearly all round the bay, repeated by the sailors, the curious, and the townspeople, who hastened out of their houses to watch the scene from the terraces. All the boats started at once, making the same tacks and rushing towards the indicated spot, like so many birds of prey. The water of the bay quivered around us as if they were beaten by the oars, and excited, as it seemed, by the general movement and enthusiasm. It soon proved, however, to be a false alarm: the pilchards had certainly shown themselves at the mouth of the bay, but had turned back, and, as if they had felt the nets, adroitly retreated to the rocks and deep waters, leaving on the trembling surface of the waves a luminous flash. As pursuit under such conditions would have been madness, it was given up. We therefore humbly resumed our positions at the end of the bay, and in sight of the hills where the post of observation was.

Two days passed thus. On the third the same signal was given from the cliffs, with white bushes. There was the same eagerness and the same tumult in the bay. This time the school of pilchards had advanced so far into the sand that it might be attacked with every prospect of success. Three men then *discharged* the nets, with the flashing rapidity of fire-arms, round the startled fish, some of which tried to turn aside, but were at once repulsed by the boats toward the mass already half enveloped by the seine. These nets are generally 160 fathoms long, and eight or ten fathoms in depth. Artistically arranged they describe a fatal circle, and enclose an entire legion of pilchards as in a ditch. The moving prison has now to be fixed by grappling hooks or anchors. This is called, in the technical language, mooring the seine. Joy at once spreads over every face. Getting into small boats the fishermen try to form an idea of the extent of the booty, and to count the number of prisoners by the size of the circle in which they are writhing. The fish from this moment are fairly caught, but they are not drawn out of the water at once. It sometimes happens that the seine will contain four or five millions of pilchards: who could raise all this mass at once? When the school is large, hours, even days, elapse ere all can be taken out, and the difficulty then is to keep them alive in their tomb, where they are pressed against one another. Boats furrow the surface of the bay, and by means of a net much smaller than the seine, and called a tucking net, the men, so to speak, skim the school of pilchards and throw them into boats, which, when full, at once return to the shore. This operation has received the name of tucking, from the second net.

The fish thus recaptured are received on shore by women and girls, who at once proceed to the operation of curing. This is another scene of movement and activity. The number of pilchards caught in St. Ives Bay is sometimes large enough to fill 34,000 barrels. It is true that I am alluding to very good years, and that in others these barrels remain absolutely empty. At such times famine spreads through the poor quarters of the town.

It may be said of Cornwall that it has three crops—one that turns golden head on the surface of the soil, another that is gathered in the gloom of the mines, and the last that ripens at the bottom of the sea. Of these three crops, the fishery is not the most fruitful, and yet its produce must not be disdained. In 1847 the pilchard crop amounted to 41,623 hogsheads. In 1862, a poor year, there were exported to the coasts of the Mediterranean and Adriatic, 17,854 barrels of pilchards, each representing a value of from fifty to sixty-five shillings.

These material results are not the only ones that should be regarded. Fishing supports on the western coast of England a vigorous population, and noble characters, formed in the hard school of incessantly recurring dangers. The education of the fishermen, I allow, is not very extensive. They have only studied two books, the Bible and the sea. In the Bible these men of simple faith learn all they want to know about the marvels of creation and their future destiny; the sea, which a Cornish poet calls the queen of serious lessons, teaches them, on the other hand, to command themselves, to wrestle against the elements with the indomitable energy of coolness, and to succour when necessary ships assailed by a storm. A great number of life-boats are stationed on the stern Cornish coast, directed by the hands of these intrepid men, who thus produce the divine simile of hope, even amid the terrible and sanguinary flashes of the lightning.

CHAPTER VI.

GENERAL STATE OF THE ENGLISH COAST—SHIPWRECKS—EXMOUTH—DEVON AND CORNWALL ARCHERY COMPANY—THE COASTGUARD STATION—A WATERING-PLACE—THE LIFE-BOAT HOUSE—THE BIRD AND THE LIFE-BOAT—LIONEL LUKIN AND MR. GREATHEAD—JAMES BEECHING—THE MARGATE LIFE-BOAT—THE SAMARITANO—THEORY OF AN INSUBMERSIBLE BOAT—THE AIR CHAMBERS—SELF RETURN—DISCHARGE OF THE WATER—A LIFE-BOAT AT SEA—THE CARRIAGE—A CORNISH LEGEND—THE LIFE-BOAT STATIONS—AN HEROIC SCHOOLMASTER—A PREACHER'S REMARK—CHARACTER OF THE CORNISH COAST—THE BELLS OF BOSCASTLE—BUDE—BAROMETERS—ADMIRAL FITZROY—THE ROCKET APPARATUS.

THE Board of Trade annually presents to the English Parliament a wreck chart, with the map of the British seas studded with black dots. Each of these dots represents a disaster, a tomb opened at the bottom of the abyss, frequently for hundreds of persons. They might be called the stores of death. This return shows that in 1863, one thousand six hundred and two shipwrecks took place on the coasts of the United Kingdom. Who can be astonished at this? The sea is the highway of the English. Four thousand vessels annually leave the coasts or enter the ports of the British Isles. These coasts are dangerous, and frequently visited by storms. One must have lived there to know what is the violence of the unchained winds. Even in the interior you are not protected from these blasts. England, it has been said, is a great vessel. The October and December gusts, the furious equinoctial gales, roar among the chimney pots of the towns as through the rigging of a storm-tossed ship. It seems as if you hear the sighs of the dying amid the clamour of the waves passing through the night. Mothers then tremble for a son, girls for a lover, nearly all for some beloved being whose life is menaced; for where is the Englishman who has not some of his family at sea? After each of these storms a cry of desolation and terror runs along the British coast. How many shipwrecks? how many lives lost?—gloomy questions, which the newspapers soon answer. The tragedies of the sea here arouse a poignant interest in all classes of society.

These catastrophes have given origin to a noble institution which exists nowhere but in England, the Life-boat Society. Our neighbours gave this name to a boat specially constructed to save the life of shipwrecked persons. Storms and the most awful seas are unable to terrify such a boat. What are the characteristics of the life-boat? How is the institution that directs them organized? What heroic services have they lately rendered? These are the questions I propose answering.

It was at Exmouth that I studied for the first time the mechanism of a life-boat. This town, situated on the Devon coast, stands, as its name indicates, at the mouth of the river Exe, where it is divided into two distinct parts, the old and the new, which are blended, however, in what may be called the harmony of contrasts. The Old Town, situated in a sandy valley, was, 150 years ago, a mere fishing village. This old quarter is still composed of narrow streets, yards, and obscure alleys, in which boatmen and sailors live. The New Town, though attached to the old one by streets of a mixed character, which form a species of transition, spreads out to the north-west on the side of a hill facing the sea. It is composed of mansions and elegant houses, standing one above the other, in clumps of trees. These pretty villas choose, with thorough English liberty, their prospect, and often the climate that suits them best. A steep, pebbly road led me between two white walls to the top of this hill, when I was surprised to find behind the town a remarkably fresh landscape, the richness of the vegetation no where announcing the vicinity of the sea. Shady lanes open out here and there between two quickset hedges, festooned with honeysuckle, eglantine, and wild clematis.

In one of these avenues, bordered by tall trees,

a young lady, with a round hat on her head, an unstrung bow in her hand, and the pockets of her dress full of arrows, advanced toward me with the assurance and mien of the hunting Diana. She entered the archery ground—a green lawn surrounded by palings, and devoted to the bow and arrow. Here she cleverly sent several arrows at a large round target, in the centre of which stood out a large black dot, like the ball of a Cyclopœan eye. The inhabitants of Cornwall and Devon were formerly valiant archers. They have retained the habit and use of this weapon, not of course as a means of defence, but as a manner of sport. Thus they form a select society, known by the name of the Devon and Cornwall Archery Company.

On the side of the town, one of the slopes of this hill descends steeply to the sands with which the mouth of the Exe is silted. You thus find yourself suddenly in presence of a great river, nearly a mile and a half wide, and forcing its way with difficulty to the ocean which repulses it. At one of the points nearest the sea is a signal post with a flag-staff. Here, in a nook surrounded by white stone and paved with black sea pebbles, a man, dressed in a waterproof cape and a round hat, watches day and night, holding in his hand a telescope, which he turns toward the different points of the horizon. His duty is to look out for ships displaying signals of distress. Behind this maritime station are seventeen houses, brilliant in their whiteness, and inhabited by twenty-three coast-guardsmen. In the centre of this small colony is the common building, where the coast-guards assemble for service, and in which they keep their weapons, in a glass case bearing the inscription "England expects that every man will do his duty." These were Nelson's own words before the battle of Trafalgar. From the windows of this house and the platform surrounding it the eye surveys a prospect possessing immense and powerfully marked lines. On one side extend the sea and the belt of coast bristling with bold promontories, among which rises Berry Head, a gloomy point that has sustained for centuries a perpetual contest with the waves; on the other side extends, for an infinite distance, the winding course of the Exe, here commanded by cultivated land, there by arid strips, or hills clothed in a tawny vegetation. One of the great features is Halden Chain, which forms a background to the picture, with its mountainous peaks. Southward, this horizon appears still more striking, owing to the elongated shadows of the cliffs, while the ruddy light of the setting sun falls on the wide and melancholy surface of the river, which is invaded by sand-banks that slacken and impede the solemn course of the slothful waters.

The coast-guard station is here the most

favourable spot to form an idea of the general appearance of the town, built on the last bend which the Exe describes before decidedly falling into the sea. This natural situation was fortunately chosen, but it has been embellished by art. The banks on which now stand the parade and other fashionable quarters of the town were in great measure conquered from the water at the beginning of this century. The pretty Heason Walk, a sort of hanging garden with verdant trees and shrubs, was cut by Lord Rolle's orders on the barren side of an old cliff. A wall, 1,800 feet in length, a gigantic work of maritime architecture such as the English know how to construct in these favourite towns, has been built to keep out the river, which is subject to tidal influences. This wall defies the return of those inundations which have more than once desolated the low-lying parts of Exmouth. Being a watering-place, the same contrast which we notice between the rich and poor districts is found again on the beach, which the townspeople and strangers like to visit. From the upper town descend male and female bathers, who, dressed in costly stuffs and eccentric costumes, offer to the waves their long tresses of perfumed hair. The lower town is represented, on the other hand, by poor women with robust limbs, who, dressed in heavy robes of blue serge, with bare feet on the sand, and faces bronzed by the sea breeze, let out the small bathing machines, and boldly thrust them into the foaming waters.

A little above the beach, and close to the coast-guard station, stands the life-boat house. It is a sort of shed, but built of stone, with whitewashed wall, and a varnished oak roof, glistening with cleanliness. The boat naturally occupies the middle of the hall, covered with a casing of coarse canvas, which protects it from the sun. The crew preside over its toilet with the same care that an English lady's maid displays in dressing or undressing her mistress. The veil that covers it having been removed, the life-boat appeared in all its elegance, heightened by blue and white colours, with some ornaments painted red. Dryden said that an idea was incarnated in everything, and that inanimate objects inspired us at first sight with a feeling of terror or confidence, according to the nature of the services for which they were destined. A man-of-war, for instance, however beautiful it may be, reassures us but poorly; we guess that its ornaments conceal dubious intentions, and in presence of its guns, in spite of the elegant form the bronze has assumed in the artist's hands, we feel a sort of fearful admiration, such as meeting a magnificent boa-constrictor in a virgin forest would arouse. The life-boat, on the contrary, has a benevolent look; it is the friend of man, the saviour of the shipwrecked. Everything here breathes a generous thought, and we are not surprised at the respect which sailors display for these useful boats.

The Exmouth life-boat is a present from Lady Rolle, and cost £350. The ground on which the life-boat house stands was purchased some years ago by a local committee. An annual subscription of £30, and some other small resources, suffice for the maintenance of the boat. It has been intrusted to the coast-guardsmen, who appear proud of the sacred charge. One of them was kind enough to explain to me the system of the life-boat; he was an old sailor who had been nearly round the world. He still wore the blue cloth jacket so dear to the national pride of the English, and a wide shirt collar turned down over this jacket discovered his bare neck, which seemed to defy the sea breeze.

The sparrow does not fly solely because it has wings; the swan does not cleave the waters with the lightness of a puff of foam solely because it has feet shaped like fins. Naturalists have perceived that another organic circumstance contributed to explain the flight of the sparrow and the swimming of the swan; it is because the bird has the faculty of filling itself with air, and thus reducing its specific gravity. I do not know whether this law of nature occurred to the mind of the inventors who first built English life-boats, but the analogy is evident at the first glance. It is not solely on account of its shape, or the number of its oars, that the life-boat proves lighter and is endowed with greater speed than ordinary boats; it is because, like the bird, it is, so to speak, swollen with atmospheric air. This invention is new, and does not date back for more than a century. To whom does the honour of the discovery belong? Walking one day in Hythe churchyard, I read on a tombstone the following inscription:—" Sacred to the memory of Lionel Lukin, the first man who built a life-boat; he was the inventor of this principle by which so many persons have escaped from a certain death at sea; he received a patent from the King in 1785." It would not be the first time that an epitaph lied, and I am bound to say that, in spite of this positive assertion, Lukin's claim as discoverer of the life-boat has been disputed. Lukin was a London coach-builder, who died in 1834. He certainly invented the plan, and supplied the model of a boat with air chambers; but was this boat ever exposed to a storm? This is a question which it is difficult to answer.

This discovery is attributed more justly to Mr. Greathead, a boat-builder at Shields. In September, 1789, a Newcastle ship, called the *Adventure*, was wrecked in the mouth of the Tyne. A multitude ran to the beach, and saw the vessel sink without a possibility of saving the crew. This event gave rise to a subscription, the amount of which would be paid to any one who invented a life-boat capable of braving the most furious seas. Only two competitors appeared—Wouldhan and Greathead. The committee decreed the prize to the latter, who was otherwise largely rewarded, as all the authors of useful discoveries are in England.* Greathead's boat rendered services, and underwent but slight alterations up to 1849. In December of that year, a vessel having run on Tynemouth Bar, twenty-four brave sailors manned the life-boat in order to help the wrecked. In its noble efforts against the infuriated waves the boat sank, and twenty of the crew perished. The consternation was great; but such calamities have this consolation, that they fecundate the germ of new progress. The Duke of Northumberland offered a prize of 100 guineas to any one who invented a life-boat having, among other indispensable qualities, the power of righting itself at once in the case of an upset. In response to this generous appeal, 280 plans and models were sent to Somerset House, where a committee spent six months in a minute examination of the different projects. The prize was at last awarded to Mr. James Beeching, a boat-builder of Great Yarmouth.

* The Society of Arts granted him a gold medal, Trinity House gave him £100, Lloyd's the same, and Parliament £1,200. I saw a model of Greathead's boat in the National Life-Boat Institution. It differs from the boats used now-a-days in various external features, but especially through its platform and the shape of the keel.

To the 100 guineas promised, the Duke added another 100 to execute the project. After Mr. Beeching's plans was thus built in his yard the first self-righting life-boat, that is to say, the first boat capable of resuming its original position after having been upset by a gust. This boat was purchased by the Commissioners of Ramsgate Harbour; and the history of its honourable services more than once revived in the hearts of the English the confidence which had been momentarily shaken by the Tynemouth catastrophe In five years, from 1855 to 1860, it saved the life of eighty persons. It will be sufficient to narrate one of its most noble exploits.

On February 2, 1860, the news reached the Margate coast that a Spanish brig, the *Samaritano*, caught by a squall of wind and snow, had been driven on to the dangerous sand-banks which obstruct the channel near the mouth of the Thames. The crew had tried to escape in the boat; but the oars broke, and the boat itself was overpowered by the waves. The two lifeboats belonging to Margate were launched one after the other, and in turn disabled by an indomitable sea. The only hope that remained was in the Ramsgate life-boat. The services of the latter were soon claimed; a coast-guardsman arrived out of breath, and learnt the sad result of the first attempts. This want of success discouraged nobody: all rushed toward the life-boat to occupy the post of honour in the face of danger. It started, towed by a steamer, the *Aid*, which, with steam up day and night, had been waiting the opportunity to be useful. Ever since the weather had been bad the struggle was terrible between the ocean and the two vessels; but, though at first repulsed, tossed about, and almost capsized, the steam-tug dug a path through the tempestuous sea. The position of the men in the life-boat was no less critical; heavy waves fell on the crew and froze as they fell, so that the poor wretches were chilled to the marrow. Although it was only one o'clock in the afternoon, the sky was so obscured that the two boats advanced in a sepulchral night; the steamer could not see the life-boat, and the life-boat could not see the steamer towing it. Amid this darkness, how was the wreck to be discovered? Fortunately a livid lull in the snow-storm allowed them to see to windward a signal of distress floating in the rigging. The two crews naturally proceeded toward this signal; but how many obstacles still separated them from the end of their glorious voyage! The snow still fell; the violence of the blast seemed to heighten with every moment, and the sea leapt more furiously than ever on the sands.

Still, the decisive hour had struck; the life-boat threw off the tug, and, after setting sail, went with its own strength alone to deliver the wrecked persons. The ghost of a ship appeared, disappeared, reappeared on the horizon, in the horrors of the twilight which covered the stormy face of the waters. At this moment a terrible doubt beset the minds of the brave sailors—would they not arrive too late? Might they not be risking their lives a thousand times for men who, according to all probability, had already found a tomb amid the waves? And yet not one of them hesitated. Forward, forward! At times the magical boat appeared buried beneath mountains of water, which broke into foam; it descended to the very bottom of the ocean, then reappeared ere long on the crest of the highest waves, as if it were supported by a supernatural force. As they approached the scene of the wreck, the sailors of the life-boat felt their hearts tremble. The sight of the submerged brig was of a nature to inspire a feeling of horror: lying on the sand, with a hole in its side, and its mainmast carried away, it was merely a pile of ruins. With what profound anxiety their eyes were fixed on the tangled mass of rigging, swept by the waves and a cloud of foam! Gradually they discovered a man, then two, then three, and finally the entire crew. With immense difficulty and danger twenty-seven persons were taken into the life-boat. Some of the wrecked, exhausted by eight hours of exposure, had not even the strength to get down and leap into the boat; they had to be lifted and carried on board. The last person in the rigging was a cabin-boy, who could not use his hands, which were half dead with cold. A vigorous arm seized him, and the life-boat returned, not without difficulty, from the remains of the wreck.

The Spaniards could not yet believe in their deliverance. Ignorant of the truly marvellous properties of a life-boat, they gazed in horror at the gloomy waves, which had lost none of their fury, and which would have inevitably swallowed up any other boat. On returning, the mast of the life-boat was broken by a terrible gust; it had to be hastily repaired amid the convulsions of the sea. In spite of all these obstacles the life-boat rejoined the tug, and re-entered the port of Ramsgate in this way, rejoicing in its victory.

Since the saving of the crew of the *Samaritano*, other striking circumstances have strengthened the confidence which the Ramsgate sailors place in the boat invented by Mr. Beeching. The system on which it is constructed, however, is not exactly the one that prevails on the English coasts. The Committee requested one of its members, Mr. Peake, master shipwright of Devonport Dockyard, to supply a design for a life-boat, combining the different features of the best models which had been sent to Somerset House. A life-boat was made after this design at Woolwich Dockyard, under the direction of the Lords of the Admiralty. After undergoing various trials, and being several times altered, this boat was finally presented to the Duke of Northumberland, who had three others like it built at his own cost. The life-boat suggested by Beeching, and improved by Peake, thus became the prototype of nearly all the life-boats which now struggle on the stormy coasts of Great Britain to convey aid to the wrecked.

This story of the invention enabled me better to understand the boat I had before my eyes at Exmouth. It will be sufficient to point out here the principal features that distinguish a life-boat from an ordinary boat. The English expect a life-boat to be insubmersible. The first condition to attain this object is, that the boat must be infinitely lighter than the volume of water it displaces. The English use the word buoyancy for the floating property which certain bodies plunged in a fluid possess. This faculty is more or less common to all boats; but the life-boat possesses it in an extraordinary degree, which is called extra buoyancy. This gift is obtained by fixing in the interior a certain number of air-boxes or chambers. The result of this mechanism is that, even if the life-boat were to fill with water, it would not the less continue to defy the weight of the waves through its agility. The compression of the air in the compartments, some of which extend along the sides, and even to the two ends of the boat, is the essential feature without which no life-boat can exist.

The second property of these boats is, righting themselves by virtue of an automatic power. In order to appreciate this advantage properly, it must be borne in mind that the art of navigation has not yet discovered victorious means to prevent a vessel sinking through certain assaults of the sea or from some other cause. Up to 1852, those who had to impart to boats a personal power of righting, or of self-return, as the English say, were accused of chasing chimeras; and yet, throughout Great Britain, children had long possessed a toy, called the tumbler, which obstinately rises, in whatever position it may be placed. The same physical laws applied to a boat at sea have produced the self-righting boat. The latter, after it has been turned completely over, rights itself like a live fish which had been laid on its back. The crew, hurled into the sea, then return to the boat, which, momentarily humiliated, but indomitable, is all ready to continue the contest. What is the secret of this marvellous property? While the prow and stern of the life-boat are lifted by atmospheric air, a heavy iron keel runs all along the boat, and fixes it on its centre of gravity. Owing to this opposition between the weight of the keel and the lightness of the two ends of the boat, the latter obstinately returns to its normal position amid the most agitated seas.

The third characteristic of a life-boat is the immediate discharge of any water that falls into it, or what the English call the self-discharge of water. The word sufficiently shows that the boat does this of itself. It performs this duty by the aid of various apparatus. One of the most curious is a series of very short tubes placed at the bottom of the boat, and closed by moveable valves. These valves resist the entrance of the water on which the boat rests; but, on the other hand, they open freely to let out the upper water which has entered the boat. By turns full and empty, the life-boat thus supplies a happy imitation of the cask of the Danaides.

Not satisfied with visiting the life-boat at home, I greatly desired to see it launched. I was obliged to wait some days for this. The lifeboat manœuvres once a quarter to practise the crew. The latter is composed of two coxswains and six oarsmen.[*] The first coxswain fulfils the duties of captain, and receives a fixed salary of £8 a-year. The oarsmen are paid on excursion days 3s. if the weather is fine, 4s. if the sea is rough, and most frequently a rough day is chosen in order to try their courage. This service is much sought after. The crew of a life-boat is formed, as the English say, of different hands; still a preference is generally given to fishermen. The latter are

[*] The number of oarsmen varies greatly, according to the size of the boat; there are sometimes ten, twelve, and even fourteen, oars.

more accustomed to the perils of the sea, and have risked their own lives so many times, that they have, as it were, acquired the right of saving those of others.

The life-boat impatiently awaited in its house the hour to rush to the beach. It was mounted on a four-wheeled truck of a peculiar shape, and so well adapted to all its movements that it might easily have been taken for a natural locomotive apparatus. This truck never leaves it; the life-boat rests on it day and night, like a gun on its carriage. Thanks to this system, the boat can travel both on land and sea, like amphibia; and when its services are claimed, it can be directed to that part of the coast nearest the wreck. The carriage of the Exmouth life-boat was at length dragged to the beach. There it was turned round, so that its rear faced the sea. The crew took their seats in the boat, the oarsmen by the side of the double row of oars, and the two coxswains, one at the stern, the other at the prow. Round hats and waterproof coats protected them from the spray. The boat had been, besides, fitted up exactly as if it was going to the aid of a shipwrecked vessel. There were on board a grappling-iron, an anchor, an axe, a compass, and a life-buoy. The sailors also put on cork life-belts, which keep the chest and shoulders of a fully-dressed man above the water. This apparatus has been advantageously substituted for the old air-belt. A few years ago, at Whitby, the whole crew of a boat perished, with the exception of one sailor, who had on the new talisman against the fury of the waves. Along the life-boat hung ropes in the shape of festoons; these were external life-ropes, to which the wrecked people could cling till they could be pulled on board. These ropes are so arranged that, if necessary, they can be used as a stirrup. The carriage was then hauled some distance into the sea by men and horses. Everything being ready, the coxswain gave the signal to start, and the boat, rolling on iron wheels, darted wildly into the sea.

Through its shape and the nature of its progress, a floating life-boat differs greatly from ordinary boats. Graceful and elegant, with the prow and stern raised, it flies—it skims the waves—it hardly ripples them: it might be called a bird. It is the dove of the ark going to carry hope over the surface of the waters. The idea of a boat which could not sink was long regarded as chimerical, and contemptuously ranked with other inventions which floated on the ocean of Utopias. At the present day, however, this boat exists; and in employing this word, I avail myself of the English metaphor, which imparts to these saviours of the seas a sort of fantastic life. With what suppleness and elasticity it obeys the waves which dominate it! how it seems to say to the sea: I am not afraid of you! It plays with the waters and skims them like a nest of kingfishers supported on a hurricane. This confidence is soon communicated to the crew. At one moment the oarsmen beat in cadence the waters that open to grant them a passage, and the boat then darts along with the speed of an arrow; at another they abandon the oars, which float along the sides of the boat like the fins of a sleeping fish. Some of the men will even leap overboard into the sea, to prove to the spectators the efficiency of the life-belts. Nothing was wanting in these manœuvres but people to save. The Exmouth lifeboat can contain, if requisite, from thirty to forty persons. After exercising for two or three hours the crew returned ashore, saluted by the hearty shouts of the crowds. The sight of a lifeboat never fails to produce a throb of joy and enthusiasm in the hearts of the English.

These quarterly exercises are to life-boats what reviews are to artillery—an image and exhibition of their power. Still, the thunder of the ordnance only arouses in the conscience of the thinker the gloomy idea of necessary evils, while the life-boat is a personification of peace and concord. It calls itself the friend of all nations: English or foreigners, rich or poor, great or small, all men are equal in its sight during a tempest.

I visited several other life-boats on the coasts of Devon and Cornwall; but as these boats only differ from each other in a few modifications,* it will be useless to dwell on them.

At certain points of Cornwall an ancient superstitious belief exists. Some old men can still remember having seen in their youth an apparition which they call the death-ship. This sinister vision was always the foreboder of some chastisement, as is proved by a fact recounted by eye-witnesses. In a village near the sea there lived, several years ago, a man who had enriched himself in a dubious way. Some of his neighbours were walking one day on the cliffs at a height of several hundred feet above the sea. One of them exclaimed, "Do you see that ship near the coast?" The others looked, and really saw in the fog that then covered the face of the waters, a large, dark vessel, with black sails swollen by a breeze, though there was not a breath of air stirring. There was not a living being on deck, no one at the wheel, no one in the rigging. The coast was dangerous, owing to submarine rocks; the vessel, in its sinuous progress, seemed to glide over these shoals without touching them. It soon disap-

* At Teignmouth, for instance, the life-boat is built of iron. A remarkable fact connected with this station is, that it was founded in 1862 by the donations of English persons living at Hong-kong and Shanghai. In gratitude to these citizens, who remembered their native land at such a distance, the Society have christened the boat the *China*.

peared, and vanished in the fog. As there was no wind, by virtue of what power was it able to move? This was the question the anxious spectators silently addressed to each other. They hastened back to the village, where the first news they heard was that Mr. M——, well known to all through the ugly rumours current about him, had just died. The mysterious ship had doubtless come to fetch his soul. Whether the world in growing old becomes more sceptical, or for some other reason I am ignorant of, the death-ship has not shown itself on the Cornish coast for a long time. Among the inhabitants, some laugh at the tradition, others have entirely forgotten it. On these seas loaded with superstitions and horrors, this vessel of death has been succeeded by a boat which also seems to move by virtue of a supernatural force. It glides like a light in the darkness of the tempest, and passes between the rocks like an apparition. Its name is, on the contrary, the boat of life; it does not come to carry off the wicked, but to save the unfortunate. While the first is retiring into the fabulous shadows of the past, the second is spreading along every coast where it can render service.

Life-boats are not peculiar to Cornwall; they extend, on the contrary, like a safety-belt along all the coasts of Great Britain; but it was chiefly during a trip to Cornwall that I was enabled to see them at work. Are they not, besides, suitably stationed amid these rocks hostile to ships, in a province which, only connected with land through Devon, and bounded by savage seas, forms, as it were, a peninsula in an island?

Cornwall at the present time possesses nine life-boats. This advantage rejoices the moralist the more because the inhabitants of Cornwall formerly had a terrible reputation, and were supposed cruelly to ill-treat wrecked persons. On the coast of this province lived a dangerous race of wreckers; this was the name given to men who enriched themselves with the spoils the sea throws up after destroying a ship. These wreckers have supplied more than one character and episode to the English melodrama. Tradition represents them as inhabiting caverns dug out by the waves at the foot of the cliffs, and indulging in every sort of barbarity. There is certainly a good deal of exaggeration in these criminal legends, which novelists and playwrights have eagerly seized on; still, I collected in Cornwall facts which prove that the old wreckers did not gain their reputation in vain. A young wrecked woman was driven ashore by the violence of the waves, and tried to cling to the rock with her nails; a wrecker, prowling along the shore like a bird of prey, noticed this girl, and saw a ring glistening on the clenched fingers with which she desperately clung to the rock: he cut off the hand in order to secure the ring. The same man, finding the trade good, and shipwrecks too rare, thought about producing them. In order to gain his end, he hobbled a donkey at night, put a lantern on its back, and led it himself along the rocks that stud the north coast of Cornwall. The halting progress of the animal, purposely dragged on by its master, formed a good imitation of the plunging motion of a sailing ship. This moving light made the ships believe they were still some distance from the coast; and such an illusion attracted them at full speed towards shoals where destruction was certain.

Long before the establishment of life-boats, such infamous deeds had been repressed in Cornwall by the public conscience. Fifty years ago, the *Antony* frigate having been driven on the rocks, those who survived the wreck were protected and treated with the greatest kindness by the inhabitants of the coast. One of the latter, a humble schoolmaster, arrived on horseback at the scene of the disaster. He saw the frigate lying on her side, the waves making a clean breach over her, hurling the living and dead toward the beach, and then dragging them back into the abyss. The only way of helping the living was to advance as far as possible into the surf, and seize some of the wretches who were drowning. The new-comer did not hesitate; he dashed with his horse into the terrible cascades which broke into foam on the sand, and succeeded in saving two men. He ventured a third time among the infuriated waves, and was just on the point of seizing a third dying man by the hair, when the schoolmaster and his horse were swept away by an implacable wave. No one was able to tell me his name; 'but he left more than a name, he left an example. This example has been followed; and I could cite a thousand traits of bravery which honour the sailors, and especially the fishermen, of Cornwall. Still, it is true that the institution of life-boats has also heightened here what the English call the standard of humanity; it has created on the coasts an emulation for devotion and sacrifice.

The evil, however, was not cured in a day. There were two perfectly distinct ways of practising wrecking, as the seizure of the spoils of the wrecked was called. One, quite criminal, consisted in killing and torturing passengers who had escaped the sea, in order to take advantage of their misfortune. If such a custom ever existed in Cornwall (and unfortunately certain stories which appear authentic leave little doubt on this point), I can affirm that it ceased long ago. Another far more deeply-rooted error was, that what belongs to the sea belongs to everybody, and that if it deigns to give up a few relics after a wreck, the riches of the dead justly lapse to the living who proceed to the beach to collect them. This belief so well agreed with the interest of the living, that it found partizans in all classes of society. It is said that a minister of the gospel was about to preach in his church, when a voice shouted in the doorway, "A wreck! a wreck!" At this news all the congregation bounded from their seats, animated by the ardour of the chase. The pastor, however, managed, by eloquence and threats, to repress for a moment the exultation of his parishioners. Descending then from the pulpit, he exclaimed, "Now, brethren, let us start fair and all together." Since the time when the clergy proved themselves so tolerant about wrecking, the surveillance of the coast-guard, and wise police laws, have notably contributed, with the progress of education, to extirpate this abuse.

The life-boat houses are naturally built on the dangerous points of the coast. In this respect there is only the difficulty of situation in Cornwall. Shipwrecks in these seas, bristling with reefs, were not only very numerous some years ago, but they had a peculiarly grave character. A ship was crushed by dashing against rocks or precipices. What was this ship? Ask this of the winds, the sea, the few insignificant fragments tossing on the immensity of the waves. To die unknown is dying twice over. Such, however, has been the lot of many ships on the Cornish coast, and no one ever knew their name, their country, or the number of passengers on board. One day, a Newfoundland dog alone survived a swallowed-up ship's company; another time a negro succeeded in reaching the beach, as he was thrown up by the surf, but he died ere he could state to what ship he belonged.

The north coast of Cornwall more especially offers gigantic obstacles to navigation. This arduous coast is composed, to a great extent, of slate rocks, piled up, broken, and submerged in a sublime disorder. Slate is a capricious formation; it changes its character and nature according to the soil. I saw it on the south-west coast of Devon displaying all the coquettishness of a silk dress shot with silver, and slightly undulated by a fresh breeze. For instance, there is near Dartmouth Castle a deep and charming bay hollowed out in this delicate slate. You go down to it by steps cut in the rock, and by crossing a wooden bridge. At the bottom is a bed of golden sand, bounded on one side by the sea, on the other by a narrow circle of cliffs. At the base of one of these cliffs, so elegantly coloured and facing the ocean, there is a fountain which filters through the schistous veins of slate. By turning a copper tap, you receive into an iron cup fastened to a chain a fresh stream as limpid as crystal. This fountain is a great blessing for the people living near, who, surrounded on all sides by the sea, are almost in the position of Tantalus in the midst of the water. Hence, while I was lying on the sand, I saw a girl of about twelve years of age come from the very top of the cliff to fill her pitcher at the spring. This done, she went back again, escalading with a sure foot the large slippery blocks, leaping from one to the other, appearing and disappearing by turns behind the uneven crests, like the fairy of the rocks in the legends of the county.

Very different is the appearance of the slate on the north coast of Cornwall. Of a blackish-grey, like the wasted bark of an aged tree, it is very frequently penetrated by veins of granite, which might be taken for streams of metal escaping through a heap of scoria. Slate, that fragile matter which powders in the hand, opposes to the sea masses whose solidity arouses a sort of stupor: it forms frowning promontories, valleys of rocks, reefs—an entire plain of ruin. Seas which dash against such obstacles have necessarily been rendered notorious by shipwrecks. A legend relates that a lord of Boscastle wished one day to make a present of a merry peal of bells to the solitary church tower of Forrabury. The bells were cast in London, and sent by sea to the dangerous Cornish coasts. The captain of the ship was a skilful seaman, who had but one fault, says the chronicler, of having confidence in himself and a good breeze, instead of relying on Providence. The ship was in sight of land; it had before it the gloomy promontory of Wellapack, and the black precipices of Plack Pit, whose summit was crowned with a multitude anxious to salute the precious cargo. All at once dark clouds obscured the sky; the wind rose with a species of fury, and the ship, hurled on the reefs, was sunk by avalanches of water. Since this event, the church-bells have remained sad and silent; but on the eve of a tempest—and tempests are not rare in Boscastle Bay—many sailors declare they have distinctly heard the bells of the Lord of Boscastle ringing at the bottom of the sea.

Life-boat stations have been established along this ill-omened coast at Bude Haven, Padstow, New Quay, and St. Ives. Such spots, feared by the sailor, are naturally dear to the artist, owing to the grand character of the scenery. Bude, for instance, a humble village composed of a group of cottages, but which, for some years past, has been aspiring to become a watering-place, is built near a romantic bay, celebrated for the opposition between the sand and the rocks. This sand, pure and golden, composed in great measure of fragments of pulverized shells, has been driven and heaped up on the coast by the stormy southwest winds. The rocks belong to the carboniferous formation, and run at right angles to the beach with Titanic contortions. Stern promontories—Compass Point and Beacon Hill—spread out wide shadows over the stern waves of the

Atlantic. In calm weather this bay is delicious: the sea at high tide advances, describing foaming semicircles, which enlarge and become appeased as they invade the beach; but let a west wind begin to blow, and the spectacle at once changes. Just as wild horses take to flight before a prairie fire, the impetuous coursers of the ocean, so the sailors say, escape from the presence of these terrible winds with a loud snorting, and rush towards the barrier of cliffs at the risk of being broken on them.

At the moment when I arrived at Bude Haven the crew of the life-boat had just gained a victory. On September 1st, 1863, the barque *Conflict* was seen at sea with signals of distress flying. It was going from Plymouth to Bristol, when it was caught by a gale off Trevose Head. The intrepid sailors at once launched the life-boat, and brought off the owner of the ship. This life-boat has rendered many other services as well. All along the coast I picked up traits of heroism which honour the institution, and also dark stories of shipwrecks. Near Padstow, a small fishing town, the brigantine *Padema* and the schooner *Betsy*, one hailing from Brixham, the other from Plymouth, having been both caught in a tremendous gale and a heavy sea, were driven, on March 18th, 1862, upon the Doon's-Bar Sand. Sand is the scourge of these districts: on land it buries churches, at sea it devours vessels. The

Padstow life-boat, which is christened after the Prince of Wales, the *Albert Edward*, was bravely launched and returned in triumph : it had saved thirteen men.

An excellent barometer is attached to the different life-boat stations ; the daily indications of the instrument are also carefully noted, so that sailors and fishermen, before going to sea, can consult the different movements of the mercury within a certain time. These barometers are submitted beforehand to Mr. Glaisher, a learned astronomer at Greenwich Observatory. In several cases such diagrams have warned the sailors of the approach of a storm which would probably have swallowed them up if, in ignorance of the danger, they had been so unfortunate as to leave port. Convinced, moreover, that the violent perturbations of the sea form a regular element in the general constitution of our planet, the English have lately sought eagerly for the law of these great meteorological phenomena. Their ambition has been, as they say, to discover the chart of the winds.

One of the boldest in this system of observations was undeniably Admiral Fitzroy, who has died recently in a fit of mental derangement, owing to severe application to the studies imposed by his enormous task. His system is based on the direction of the aerial currents. Sometimes currents of air circulate side by side for hundreds and thousands of miles, but following opposite directions, like railway trains crossing each other on two parallel lines; at other times they lie upon each other, or frequently cross at unequal angles; other times they combine, and by joining their forces produce those variations of atmosphere so frequent when the wind blows from the equator or from the nearest pole. Such is occasionally the antagonism of these currents in their angular collision, that they give rise to wide tornadoes, a sort of revolving storm, which is the most terrible of all in the whole world. Admiral Fitzroy's calculations consist in predicting the arrival of one of these atmospheric currents at a given station. The news is then communicated by telegraph to all the points threatened along the coast. Telegraphing a storm is a pretension which still finds unbelievers, I am bound to add. However this may be, alarm or caution signals, which are now quite familiar to sailors, are at once hoisted at all the naval stations. These signals consist chiefly of a cone and a drum, both made of coarse canvas painted black, and lined inside with hoops. The storm drum indicates the event; the cone, which is placed over the drum, announces the probable direction of the wind which may be expected. In the case of the danger being imminent, a second cone is added. At night the signal is given by means of lights placed in triangles or squares. Admiral Fitzroy was a sort of meteorological minister; he had at his orders a staff, a budget, and the electric wires. His system costs the State £5,800 a year. The art of reading the elements is only proved by facts, and these facts have been sufficiently numerous to inspire English sailors at any rate with real confidence. When they notice the drum floating in the sky, those of them who were on the point of weighing anchor let it fall again heavily on the bed of the port, and wait till the danger is past.

Life-boats are not the only safety apparatus existing in England. Certain Cornish coasts, for instance, are so studded with rocks, among which the sea boils, that the best boat incurs the greatest dangers and can render but slight service. Most frequently, too, ships are lost near the shore, among the reefs which defend it. In the latter case recourse is had to what are called life-lines. These lines are sent from shore either by means of a mortar or a rocket. The mortar is placed on the shore, and loaded with a shell aimed at the rigging of the ship which displays signals of distress. A fine line is rolled up at the mouth of the mortar, and follows the flight of the shell, like a thread fastened to a bird's leg.

If, on the other hand, a rocket is fired, the effect is precisely the same, and the latter can reach a distance of 300 yards. The crew of the ship in danger seize the line entangled in the rigging and fasten it to a larger rope, which is dragged ashore by the men who have undertaken to afford help. In this way a communication is established between the ship and the coast. This rope, just stretched out in an inclined position, forms a sort of bridge. By means of a pulley or running knot, a basket is placed on it, into which the wrecked people enter in turn, generally by threes, and it reaches land by a natural movement of gravitation, and by the manœuvres of the crew or the men collected on the coast. An eye-witness of this ingenious method of saving life described to me one day his emotion at the sight of a mother and two children thus launched in a basket amidst a horrible tempest. Like a frightened dove collecting its young under its wings, the unhappy woman wrapped her children in her arms, and drew them to her heart; it seemed as if she wished to save them from the brutal and ferocious waves which rose with the roaring of savage monsters round this fragile nest. Three hundred and twenty-nine persons were saved in 1863, all over England, by the rocket apparatus.

The life-boat stations are managed and supported by local committees; but most of the committees are under the control and patronage of the National Life-boat Institution, whose seat is in London. Elsewhere we should expect to find such a service of public utility organized by the State. In England, the State has undertaken the material defence of the coasts; it raises batteries, builds forts, and forms a sanitary cordon of custom-house officers against the evils of smuggling. It has to some extent accepted the ungrateful part of the task, while it yielded the generous part to individual efforts. The National Life-boat Institution receives nothing from the Government, and depends solely on public charity. At its offices we shall be better able to comprehend the unity of a system of which we have as yet only seen the scattered members at work.

CHAPTER VII.

ORIGIN OF THE LIFE-BOAT SOCIETY—SIR WILLIAM HILLARY—DECADENCE AND RECOVERY OF THE SYSTEM—A FORTUNATE CATASTROPHE—CHARACTER OF THE DONATIONS—THEIR MOTIVES—THE BUDE HAVEN LIFE-BOAT—NUMBER OF PERSONS RESCUED SINCE THE FOUNDATION OF THE SOCIETY—THE DISASTER AT SCARBOROUGH IN 1861—MEDALS AND HONORARY CERTIFICATES—JAMES M'MILLAN—A PROCESSION FOLLOWING A LIFE-BOAT—RECEIPTS OF THE SOCIETY—THE OFFICERS AND SECRETARY—EXPENSES OF THE COMPANY—THE VICTORIES OF PEACE.

ABOUT 1823 terrible shipwrecks had desolated the coasts of England. There lived at that time in the Isle of Man a baronet, Sir William Hillary, who resolved to prevent, or at least to attenuate, the consequences of maritime disasters. He was not rich; his fortune had been lost in the West Indies, and also in Essex, where he had equipped at his own expense several volunteer regiments at the time when the first Napoleon threatened to invade Great Britain. Instead of money, he had noble aspirations and a firm intellect. His generous appeal on behalf of the shipwrecked sailors found a response in the heart of a wealthy London merchant, Mr. Thomas

Wilson, M.P. The richest city merchants entered into the views of the latter gentleman, and declared their readiness to open their purses. Lord Liverpool, the Premier, encouraged Mr. Wilson; but faithful to English traditions, he refrained from pledging the State to a work which must be entirely supported by free sympathies.

Early in 1824 a public meeting was held at the London Tavern. Dr. Manners Sutton, Archbishop of Canterbury, presided over this meeting, at which were also noticed Wilberforce and Lord John Russell, who was then entering public life. Mr. Wilson was nominated president of the society; and as the Northumberland coast had the melancholy honour of being celebrated for the number and gravity of its wrecks, the institution established the first life-boat station there. A boat was also stationed at the Isle of Man. Sir William Hillary, who suggested the idea whence the Life-boat Society sprang, ventured himself several times into this boat, and saved more than one shipwrecked man. One day he all but perished: having been hurled out of the boat by the tempest, he broke several ribs, and never completely recovered from the effects of this accident. The country was at that time suffering from a commercial crisis, and the interest apparently at first taken in the Life-boat Institution seemed to subside. Several of the local associations died a natural death, as the English say. For want of inspection, the boats got out of order. Besides, what could an institution effect with an income of £400 or £500 a year? As it no longer acted, it was forgotten. There were hardly a dozen life-boat stations throughout the kingdom, and yet shipwrecks multiplied with the increasing number of vessels.

Such was the state of decadence among the life-boats, when a frightful disaster in 1849 led to the regeneration of the establishment. Twenty Shields sailors perished in sight of the coast. This sad event dragged the society out of its long sleep. In the following year the Duke of Northumberland was nominated its president; the committee was rearranged, and Mr. Richard Lewis undertook to remodel, as secretary, a service which entirely lacked direction. Everything has changed since that moment. Without attempting to encroach on the liberty of the local committees, the Institution entered into relations with them, and through one of its officers exercised an active surveillance over all the life-boat stations that were willing to be attached to a centre. It also established a fixed rate of pay for the coxswains, and for the crews of the life-boats a system of remuneration proportioned by the nature of the services. The result of these efforts was to lead back to the society the sympathy which had left it. The

English do not like to give their money for good actions badly performed; but, so soon as they see a generous object and effective means to attain it, they are not niggardly in their charity. It is calculated that nearly £4,000,000 are annually paid by private persons to the several charitable societies. With such a budget, benevolence constitutes among our neighbours what would be called in France "a state within a state."

The Institution now possesses 132 life-boats, distributed along the most dangerous coasts of England. Each of these boats costs, with its accessories, from £500 to £600; hence, if we only regard it from a material point of view, a very considerable capital is floating amid the tempests. Doubtless Great Britain may be proud of vessels much more haughty and much more expensive —real cities of iron or wood which raise their masts triumphantly on the surface of the waves, like the steeple of a church; but though the English navy is so admirable, the sight of this humble fleet, excellently equipped, ever ready, and animated to some extent by the love of humanity, possesses a grandeur of its own.

A lady called one day at the offices of the Society, and left the money necessary to purchase a life-boat, while refusing to make her name known. She returned thrice again, and at each visit deposited the price of a new life-boat. "I shall be amply rewarded," she said, "if I ever hear that one of these four boats has saved the life of a single person." Her wish was granted. During the winter of 1862, a fearful storm broke out at night in Dundrum Bay. At daybreak, a wretched man was seen clinging to the rigging of a sunken ship. An ordinary boat, which was on the coast, bravely advanced to help him; but it was soon upset by the surf, and the six men forming its crew had great difficulty in escaping. Fortunately there was in Dundrum Bay one of the life-boats given by the lady without a name, as she had been christened. The boat put to sea, soon reached the scene of the shipwreck, and took out of the rigging the unfortunate man, who gave no sign of life, but speedily recovered from his state of insensibility when he found himself on land again. He was the skipper of the boat; and he stated that his crew, composed of three men, had been washed overboard during the nocturnal storm.

Frequently these voluntary donations of life-boats are inspired by a feeling of gratitude. About four years ago, the yacht of a noble lady, who was visiting the coast of Ireland, was run down by a fishing lugger. The lady was saved by one of her friends, who, diving and swimming, carried her ashore. As a sort of *ex voto*, she offered the Institution £300 to establish a new life-boat on the Irish coast. This boat was stationed at Carnsore, a poor village near the

Wexford rocks. In the following winter the *Guyana* of Glasgow was disabled off Carnsore by a frightful sea. The life-boat given to Carnsore was at once launched into the tempest, and nineteen wrecked men, who had been exposed for upwards of five hours to all the insults of the sea and all the agony of an imminent death, were carried to land safe and sound.

On other occasions it is to a noble feeling of domestic reverence that the life-boat owes its origin. Not long ago a visitor called at the offices of the Institution to offer a life-boat, which he proposed to maintain by a perpetual donation in memory of his mother. I saw at Budehaven, in Cornwall, a memorial of this description, inspired by the same touching thought. The following inscription was engraved on a stone slab in the wall of the boat-house:—

<blockquote>
IN MEMORY OF
ELIZABETH MOORE GARDEN,
THE BELOVED WIFE OF
ROBERT THEOPHILUS GARDEN,
THIS LIFE-BOAT
WAS OFFERED TO
THE NATIONAL LIFE-BOAT INSTITUTION
BY THEIR CHILDREN.
</blockquote>

This boat was launched for the first time on June 19th, 1863, the birth-day of Elizabeth Garden, whose memory this life-boat was intended to perpetuate. It was the custom in the middle ages to build chapels for the repose of the souls of the dead. The English, since the Reformation, no longer believe in the efficacy of prayers for the dead; but if these souls still take an interest in earthly things, what purer joy could be afforded them, what testimony more worthy of immortal beings, than to attach their names to these liberators of the sea? May we not say that the divine breath of humanity swells the sails of such boats, which carry through the darkness and the lightning consolation to the heart of those who are despairing?*

Does the efficiency of the life-boats entirely respond to the noble intentions of the founders? This is a question easy to answer by figures. Since 1824, when the Society was founded, up to 1863, the life-boats saved 13,568 persons. The year 1863 was notorious for the number of shipwrecks. The autumn gales were, perhaps, the most destructive of all those that ever desolated the British coasts. In the towns of Yarmouth and Shields, widows and children whom the storm of December left behind it may be counted by

* As a general rule, the field of charity is divided in the erection of a life-boat station. One person furnishes the boat, a second buys the land on which it rests, and a third builds the house to shelter it. The life-boat work is thus a collective task in which each helps in proportion to his means. Frequently, too, towns club together to provide the expense of such establishments: in 1862 Ipswich collected £500, which it sent to the Life-Boat Society; and, in 1863, Bath, though not a seaport, offered £248 to establish a life-boat on the coast of the Bristol Channel.

hundreds. Amid so many calamities 4,565 persons escaped the waves that yawned to swallow them up: 498 of these were succoured by lifeboats, 329 by the rocket apparatus, and 3,738 either by the boats of the wrecks themselves, by steamers, or by fishing-boats. It must be remarked that the 498 rescues effected by the lifeboats constituted what are called, in medical and maritime language, desperate cases. According to all probability these persons could not have been saved by any other intervention. The lifeboats form, in the army of deliverance, a sort of reserved body or sacred battalion, which proceeds to the most menaced parts of the battle, and encourages by its exploits the ardour of the other combatants.

Another consideration which operates powerfully in favour of the life-boats, properly so called, is the small number of accidents that has happened to the men who manage them. Everybody knows, however, how dangerous it is to approach the scene of a wreck through a sea agitated by all the furies of the tempest. In such a case no boat is insured against peril; there are no human inventions which can always resist certain revolts of the elements. The lifeboats themselves, I am bound to add, have experienced this truth. But where would be the merit of the crew if the devotion of the men was not sometimes subjected to terrible proofs?

What they have seen on these awful seas they alone could describe. The most powerful organizations do not always resist these mournful scenes, these violent shocks of the deep. Some of them have been attacked in consequence by nervous crises which help them to the tomb. Amidst such terrible circumstances the Institution has had but very rare catastrophes to deplore. I will confine myself to describing one that took place on November 3rd, 1861.

Between four and five o'clock in the afternoon, the schooner *Coupland* was proceeding with a cargo of granite from Aberdeen to Scarborough: but it was in vain that it tried to enter the port; its masts were carried away, it was repelled by waves chasing each other like a herd of savage buffaloes, and hurled upon a sand-bank that stretches out in front of the Spa, a promenade of the town. The life-boat, however, was already at sea, and flying to succour the crew of the schooner, who were exposed to the greatest danger. The weather was awful; the sea beat against the Spa wall with such violence that the stones of the parapet were dislocated. The rebound of the waves, moreover, produced such a rolling, that no other boat but an English life-boat could have supported it. The crew of the life-boat could be seen, and even spoken with, from the promenade. A tumult of emotions and cries of agony ran along the whole line of the quays, when the crew themselves appeared struck with terror. At one moment the boat was furiously hurled against the stone bar, at another it was swallowed up in foaming cataracts. A terrible shock threw the coxswain into the sea —Thomas Clayburn, a brave veteran, who, being carried towards the Spa wall by the movement of the waves, was succoured by the aid of a life-belt. Three other men were in turn thrown out by the blows and furious bounds. The raging waves tore the oars from the hands of the rowers, who were thus disarmed against the wrath of the ocean. The unhappy men threw out lines on to the promenade, which, being at once seized by powerful hands, served to tow the boat through the surf to a landing-stairs at the northern end of the wall. As soon as the boat touched land the men leaped out ere the waves had retired. Seeing the danger they were incurring, a great number of persons rushed forward to assist them. Here began a scene of confusion and disasters, in which several inhabitants of the town and two of the crew lost their lives. One of them was killed by a collision of the boat, which, rising suddenly, was violently hurled against the stone wall. He fell as a dead man falls, face forward, and was swept away for ever by the waves. The other was drowned: he was the only one who had neglected to put on his life-belt. The life-boat, having no one left to manage it, was cast against the crags and destroyed. Was this a defeat? Doubtless; and the crew of the schooner had to be succoured by another safety apparatus —the rocket apparatus. It must be remarked, however, that, even under these unfortunate circumstances, the boat astonished everybody by its rare qualities. It did not capsize, and it resisted the most impetuous shocks. Accidents, however, seem more and more to spare the crews of the life-boats: during the whole of 1863, which was so big with storms and wrecks, the Institution had not the loss of a single man to deplore, and at the present time there are about 6,000 sailors attached to this service.

Not satisfied with equipping and maintaining in good order this rescuing fleet, the Society distributes rewards to all those who have distinguished themselves by their noble conduct. These rewards consist of money, medals, and honorary certificates. After each expedition to wrecks, the life-boat crew receive a sum proportionate to the nature of the danger they have incurred. The medals are of gold or silver: they bear on one side the bust of Queen Victoria, and on the reverse the image of a life-boat, in which three sailors are drawing a shipwrecked man out of the water. These medals are only decreed to persons who have seriously risked their lives in saving those of others. A minute inquiry is made before the Committee forms a decision, and all the circumstances connected with the shipwreck are laid before it. The result is that these rewards—the gold medal more especially—are only granted in extraordinary cases, and for services which really arouse admiration.

The Society does not restrict its gifts and honours to the men it employs in the life-boats; it has also undertaken what may be called the education of devotion. It teaches men to become brave; it teaches them to risk themselves for their fellow-men: at least the English believe so, and they have thus opened a species of school of sacrifice. In this way the Institution exerts an influence over the whole navy of Great Britain. It is to some extent interested in the deliverance of those whom it does not save directly by means of its boats. Fishermen who have launched their boats to save the shipwrecked, intrepid swimmers who have seized a dying man in the raging waves; all those, in a word, who have displayed great courage, have a claim to the distinctions and thanks of this impartial jury. No class of British society regards itself as above such rewards. After the Scarborough accident, Lord Charles Beauclerk, Mr. William Tindall, son of a banker of the town, and Mr. John Fley, having nobly perished in attempting to help the crew of the life-boat, the Committee presented a silver medal to their families.

On other occasions simple workmen receive

similar honours. I was at Campbelton, a small town of Kantyre, on the south coast of Scotland, when a public meeting was held to present a medal granted by the National Life-Boat Institution to James McMillan, a poor artizan, upwards of seventy years of age, who had saved several drowning persons during his life. A short time previously he had brought ashore a sailor of the *Genoa*, a merchant vessel, which a storm destroyed on October 13th, 1862. The meeting was enthusiastic; and to furnish an idea of the interest attaching throughout the United Kingdom to such acts of courage, I will quote a few of the remarks of Mr. Stewart, the chairman:— "James," he said, "I knew your father; he lived on my father's estate and on mine. Everybody considered him a strong man and a brave man. He never raised his arm in his own cause, but more than once he raised it in behalf of others, and especially in the defence of the weak. If his arm was strong to strike, it was also strong to help. You, James, his son, have inherited from him this disposition to risk your life to preserve that of others. This is not the first time that you have proved worthy of your father. You saw this man clinging feebly to a rock; you also saw him loose his hold. It was all over with him if an heroic hand had not come to his succour; he would infallibly have been carried away by the back-wash. While others looked on, and among them young men, you rushed into the raging waves, and with your strong arm and noble courage brought him safe to land. Heaven aided you; it protects the brave! James, your conscience has already told you how great a thing it is to snatch the life of a brother from the dangers and horrors of that night—from a death amid the waves. I shall say no more about it. Take this parchment, on which the National Life-Boat Institution has recorded its opinion of your noble conduct. Another gentleman will fasten the medal on your chest. Long after you are lying in the ground your sons will see that medal. It will remind them of what you were, and it will excite them and their children to deeds of compassion, courage, and devotion."

It is easy to comprehend the moral effect of such meetings on the coast population. Men have made a flag out of a rag by attaching to it the idea of honour; why shall not the sail torn by the tempest not become also an appeal and a signal for those who love glory?

As the Institution exists on public liberality, it has been obliged necessarily to arouse the national sympathy in favour of the sailor and the wrecked. It has recourse to everything that can affect the heart and the imagination: to music, poetry, engraving, and publicity. Thanks to this fortunate assistance of literature and the fine arts, the life-boat has become in the mind of the masses a sacred object, a palladium of the seas. Two years ago I remember following in the streets of London a procession which was triumphantly conveying to the Thames a new life-boat for Tynemouth. Fifty sailors belonging to the Royal Naval Reserve opened the march, with a band at their head. The boat was drawn on its carriage by four magnificent horses. Volunteers in uniform accompanied the procession, and along the road the crowd displayed a sort of enthusiastic respect for an institution which offers its services to the whole world, irrespective of rank, religion, or nationality. It was not, I acknowledge, the stirring entry of Garibaldi into London, but it was not the less an ovation. In those seaport towns where the life-boat appears for the first time, the bells are rung, the cannon roar, and pocket-handkerchiefs are waved. It is this moral force of opinion which opens the source of the voluntary gifts and subscriptions.

The total receipts of the Society in 1863 amounted to £21,101 6s. 3d. Among these donations some are distinguished by a real magnificence: a London house, that of Messrs. Cama and Co., Parsee merchants, gave £2,000. There are others which have an affecting character: "5s. from a child's saving-box;" "£20 offered by a sailor's daughter, the earnings of her needle;" "£100 given by a stranger to thank God for having saved his life at sea during the storm of October 31st, 1863."

Foreign Governments have also frequently shown their gratitude to the Society for services rendered to their sailors by the English life-boats. On October 20th, 1862, the *Annie Hooper*, a large American ship bound from Baltimore for Liverpool, was trying to force the entrance of the Mersey, towed by a steamer, when the captain and pilot, meeting with an invincible resistance, thought it prudent to get out to sea: but the ship had become unmanageable; driven by wind and tide, it was cast ashore at Southport. The mountains of water and foam hid its critical situation for a while. At last the signals of distress were perceived at Southport and Lytham, two points where there are fortunately life-boat stations. The two boats started to do their duty. Such was the frightful state of the sea, however, that the boats, usually so swift, took four hours and a half in going a distance of four miles. After incredible efforts the whole crew of the American ship—that is to say, eighteen persons, including the pilot, who belonged to Liverpool—was saved by the two life-boats. President Lincoln, on hearing of the danger his countrymen had incurred and the heroic manner in which they had been delivered, sent £100 to the Institution and £31 to the crew of the two boats. The pilots of Liverpool proved no less generous; they made a subscription and gave £14 to the Lytham life-boat, in gratitude for the service rendered to one of their comrades. We thus see how the treasury of the Society is supported; on one hand, those who owe their lives to it, on the other, those who are animated by a disinterested feeling of compassion for accidents of the sea, contribute to support an institution regarded by all as one of the glories of Great Britain.

The seat of the Society is at John Street, Adelphi, in London, where it occupies a locality in no way distinguished externally from a private house. The English are fond of doing great things in small houses. The administration is divided into two very distinct branches—the Committee, which, as it were, represents the legislative power, and the officers, who, under the direction of Mr. Richard Lewis, secretary of the Institution, perform the executive duties. The secretary's room is a large hall, in which there is a collection of models of the principal systems of life-boats since the origin of the invention. The walls are decorated with pictures and photographs, representing the life-boat stations and scenes of shipwrecks. Over the mantel-piece is the wreck chart, published annually by the Board of Trade, and which the Institution also republishes on a smaller scale, except that by the side of the black dots representing disasters it places red crosses which indicate the life-boat stations.

The duties of the Committee are performed gratuitously; the officials alone are paid, but within the most economical limits: the salaries of the secretary, clerk, and book-keeper do not exceed £670 a-year. The business of the latter consists in receiving the money paid by subscribers, and paying the expenses of the establishment and the keeping up of the life-boats. The management is thus perpetually in communication with the provincial committees: it is a link between the centre and the branches; it controls their movements without oppressing them at all, so as to establish unity in liberty. The radius over which the surveillance of the administration spreads is very extensive, as it embraces England, Scotland, and Ireland; but an ingenious system of correspondence greatly simplifies the duties of the office. The latter sends to all the life-boat stations printed slips containing a list of queries relating to the state of the boats, the payment of the crew, and the exercising on stormy days. These slips are returned covered with answers, and thus serve as a basis for the labours of the secretary. The management has also under its orders an inspector—a man of great experience and possessed of very extensive knowledge—Captain J. R. Ward, whose duty it is to visit along the coasts the different branches of the life-boat system. By the aid of all these combined elements, the secretary annually presents to the Committee, which meets at the London Tavern, a general report of the pecuniary position of the Society, the services rendered, and the rewards voted: this report obtaining the greatest publicity through the newspapers. The administration of the life-boats is, to use the expression of an Englishman, a glass charity box, in which the enlightened eye of charity can follow the march of the widow's mite, and thus judge the manner by which it is converted into useful works.

Out of receipts amounting to £21,101 6s. 3d. the Society spent in 1863, £16,672 6s. 8d. It is little when we reflect how much a fleet of war costs the State. The pacific fleet of the life-boats also has its victories: it is when the tempest bursts forth, when the thunder roars, when night and wind spread out over the sea, that it rushes eagerly into the fray. After victories gained over an enemy on the field of battle, the dead are counted; after the victories of the life-boats over the furies of the deep, the living are counted. Not satisfied with saving shipwrecked persons itself, the Institution has been for some time engaged in generalising the means of succour. Employing for this purpose its influence over the mercantile marine, it invites them to substitute for the heavy boats carried by ships, and which never save anything, real life-boats built on the principles of the Society. In seaports and fishing villages it proposes to introduce a new system of boats, which would at all times resist the assaults of the roughest waves. It will be easy to judge of the importance of this reform, when I state that the coasts of the United Kingdom possess about 40,000 fishing-boats managed by nearly 160,000 men ever ready to devote themselves in stretching out a hand to the shipwrecked. The life of all is sacred; but in the eyes of the English that of the sailor and the fisherman is doubly precious; first, from a humanitarian point of view, and secondly, from that of political economy. These men render services which demand a peculiar courage, and the death of one of them is a loss for the whole of society. It would require volumes to narrate their exploits; still, I may be permitted to point out some of those traits of heroism which, in recent years, have imparted a species of national interest to the attempts at rescue.

CHAPTER VIII.

THE WRECK OF THE 'FORFARSHIRE'—GRACE HORSLEY DARLING—
ELIZA BYRNE—WRECK OF THE 'ROYAL CHARTER'—JOSEPH
ROGERS—SAVING A FISHING-BOAT ON THE HARBORO' SANDS—
'THE COUNTESS OF LISBURNE'—A CORNISH FISHERMAN ABOARD
A LIFE-BOAT—A STRUGGLE BETWEEN JEALOUSY AND DUTY—
COMPARISONS BETWEEN THE MEANS OF RESCUE IN FRANCE AND
ENGLAND—HOW THE SUPERIORITY OF MODERN CIVILIZATION OVER
ANCIENT COUNTRIES IS RECOGNIZED.

On September 5th, 1838, the *Forfarshire* steamer left Hull for Dundee. It had above forty passengers, and the crew consisted of twenty-four men. The captain's wife accompanied him on the voyage. As the wind blew a gale, and the sea was rough, the rolling of the vessel injured the boiler, which was already in a bad state. The water, in escaping, put out the fire, and the engine stopped. It was then nine o'clock at night, and the vessel was off St. Abb's Head, a great promontory that rises on the coast of Scotland. The danger was in being cast ashore; hence all sail was set, and the vessel withdrew from the menacing line of the coast. A dense fog spread over the sea, so that it was impossible to tell where they were. Suddenly the breakers and lights of the Ferne lighthouse were perceived. There was no possibility of doubt that the danger was imminent. They tried to tack between the Ferne Islands, but the ship refused to answer the helm, and at about three in the morning it ran with frightful violence against the rocks of Longstone Island. At the moment when the shock took place some of the passengers were asleep in their cabins. Suddenly awakened, they rushed half-dressed on deck, which, at this moment, offered a scene of confusion and horror. The long-boat was lowered, and everybody tried to get into it; but such was the violence of the sea, that the boat parted from the ship, and several of the passengers perished in a supreme effort to cling to life.

The boat itself only escaped by a miracle. There was but one passage which it could enter without being torn in pieces by the rocks that surrounded it. The sailors knew naught of this; they had left everything to chance, that is to say, to the wind, the sea, the darkness; but the boat, guided by a sort of instinct, turned of its own accord into this narrow passage. After being exposed for the whole night to the rudest assaults of the tempest, it was picked up by a sloop which towed it into Shields. The fate of those, however, who remained aboard the steamer was deplorable; five minutes after it had been cast ashore, a second shock parted it in two. The prow alone of the vessel remained firm on the rock, and the passengers who still breathed naturally sought shelter on this fragment. Clinging to their last plank of safety, they expected every instant to share the fate of their unfortunate companions whom they had seen swept away by the waves.

Fortunately, there stands on one of these islands a lighthouse, called, from its position, the Outer Ferne, and in this lighthouse the keeper's daughter, Grace Horsley Darling, was awake on this night. She heard through the confused yells of the storm a fearful blow, and then the cries of the shipwrecked. She rose, and went to awake her father. "Father," she said to him, "do you hear those noises?" "I can hear," the old man replied, "the wind howling and the sea raging." "I," she continued, "hear voices imploring help." To launch a boat on these stormy waves seemed an insane enterprise. It was near daybreak; but the faint light which fell on the surface of the deep through the fog only served to show the immensity of the danger. The worthy keeper of the lighthouse was a man of experience, and he hesitated. His daughter rushed into the boat with an oar in her hand; but it bore no resemblance to the life-boat of the present day. The father could no longer resist; he followed her. An old man and a girl, what a poor crew to tear from the powerful waves a prey already seized and half devoured! Devotion was stronger than the tempest. With their eyes fixed on a point of the horizon, they discovered that living beings were still clinging to the relics of the wreck. The fury of the wind was still the same, and at each moment the frail skiff seemed to be rushing to certain ruin. By means of a dangerous manœuvre and a desperate effort, the couple at length reached the rock on which the vessel had been dashed. The same fate menaced the boat, and it required all the skill of the two pilots to prevent it being torn to pieces. Nine persons, five of the crew and four passengers, alone survived the disaster. The others, who had sought a refuge on the rock, had been torn away in turn by the heavy, icy waves which incessantly leapt on it. The captain and his wife were dead, closely embraced in each other's arms. A mother held in her stiff, clenched hands two children, a boy and a girl, one eight, the other twelve years of age, both suffocated long ago by the pressure of the waves. The nine survivors were taken into the boat. Pale as shadows, they gazed with silent stupor at this intrepid young woman, Grace Darling, who was taking them to land. The weather was so bad that they were unable to reach land till Sunday morning. Grace Darling sheltered inside the lighthouse the nine victims she had saved. For three days and nights she nursed them, she consoled them, and restored their hopes as she had done their lives.

This noble conduct aroused a transport of enthusiasm throughout Great Britain. Painting, music, the theatre, poetry, celebrated the horrors of this mournful night and the courage of Grace Darling. Her example was the origin of the acts of heroism which are repeated in every storm. It seems as if all the women of England feel the vibration of the generous words of Grace Darling, "Father, they are drowning, and we could save them." The Wicklow station, a branch of the London National Life-Boat Society, some two years ago advised the Central Institution to reward the devotion of Eliza Byrne, an Irish woman, who had saved a girl on the coast. The girl was bathing, when she suddenly disappeared beneath the waves. Eliza Byrne was some distance from the coast; she fastened round her waist a line, which she got another woman to hold, and then, full-dressed, rushed into the water, dived, and seized the unfortunate girl, whom she brought back to land ere the last spark of life was extinguished. This was the third person she had saved within a few years.

One of the most celebrated wrecks in England is that of the *Royal Charter*, which took place on October 25th, 1859. This steamer was bringing back to England 490 persons, when it was attacked during the night by an awful gale off the coast of Anglesey. The sea hurled it with unparalleled violence upon the rocks. A sailor, Joseph Rogers, thinking that the vessel could not long endure the weight of the waves that assailed it, resolved to save the passengers. In order to execute this plan, he leapt into the sea and began swimming ashore while uncoiling a long line, one end of which he had fastened to the condemned vessel.

In order fully to comprehend all the courage this enterprise needed, the existence of what the English call a broken sea must be known. Even though the bottom may be composed of sand and pebbles, the force of the falling waves is so great, and their back-wash so violent, that in the majority of cases they defy the strongest and most skilful swimmer. Far more terrible is the danger when the waves dash with all their fury against the sharp angles of rocks as hard as a diamond; a thousand times more awful still is the situation of the swimmer when he has darkness all around him, when fragments of wreck encumber the moving crests of the waves, and when the temperature of the water is so low as to freeze the blood in the veins of the bravest man. Joseph Rogers had to contend against all these combined obstacles; he had foreseen them, but had not hesitated for an instant. It is certainly true that he saved his own life in saving the lives of others; but if he had only thought of self, would he have loaded himself with a line, which so greatly augmented the embarrassments and difficulties of his perilous voyage? Besides, at the moment when he left the ship there was a greater chance of being rescued aboard than of reaching shore under such unfavourable conditions. A generous feeling, consequently, overpowered in Rogers the instinct of self-preservation. His efforts were crowned with success; he reached land; and a means of communication being established by the aid of a line between the ship and the shore, twenty-five persons were saved in baskets. The 490 would all have escaped death in the same way if the vessel had not broken up and sunk for ever to the bottom of the sea while the operation was being carried on. The National Life-Boat Institution granted the gold medal to the brave sailor, Joseph Rogers. He received, in addition, £5, a very poor present, doubtless, for such a service; but such deeds find their reward in the hearts of those who perform them.

The Englishman possesses, perhaps more than any one else, the sort of courage suitable for such enterprises; he has what is called *pluck*, that is to say, a firm, reflective, invincible courage, a feeling of natural bravery against evil fortune and the unchained elements. If anything could further develop in him the resources of this masculine energy, it would be assuredly compassion for the extraordinary sufferings to which the unfortunate shipwrecked are but too often exposed. On November 7th, 1859, a fishing-boat was wrecked in sight of the Norfolk coast, on the Harboro' Sands, near Bacton. As the boat had sunk, the four men composing the crew, and the boy, took refuge on the mast. For a whole day and night they had no other support but this tree, rising about eight feet above the raging sea. They were without food, and almost without clothes. One of them took off his shirt and waved it in the air as a signal of distress, but the wind tore it from his enfeebled hands. The boy, who was at the top of the mast, held out till the second day, when, exhausted with fatigue, he loosed his hold and slipped into the sea. One of the men seized him, and restored him to the position he had lost. They had nothing with which to fasten him to the mast, and no crossjacks left on which he could rest, hence, on the following night, the lad, almost insensible from cold, and with his strength quite expended, fell again : this time he was hopelessly lost.

On the morrow the shipwrecked men had a gleam of hope. A ship passing in the distance noticed their signals, heard their cries, and sent a boat to their assistance. After struggling in vain against the wind and tide, the boat gave up the trial and returned to the ship. The four wretched men thus saw every chance of a rescue vanish. A gloomy despair seized on them—they bade farewell to life. Still, they had resolved to die at their post, and frenziedly clung to the mast. One or two hours later they heard a gun fired. At this sound they regained courage; it might be a signal! A boat had in reality put out to seek them; but as they only formed a dot lost on the dark ocean, and as night was descending at this very moment on the surface of the waters, they could not be discovered. The boat sadly regained land, and the gloom grew denser over the sea.

It was the third night: they passed it like the two others, clinging to the mast-head, and fearing more and more that, as the base might give way at any moment, they would all be buried in the waves. The next morning a Bacton boat made a fresh attempt, reached them at about ten o'clock, and landed them, more dead than alive, at Palling. As soon as they were able to support the journey, they were transferred to the Sailors' Home at Yarmouth. Their swollen and stiffened limbs, their spectral pallor, their gloomy silence, all sufficiently announced the terrible trials they had undergone. It took several weeks ere they were quite recovered. The Life-Boat Institution voted £18 for the crew of the yawl which, as it were, had drawn them from the bottom of the grave.

These various exploits were accomplished by

ordinary boats: it is curious to contrast with these the conduct of the life-boats. When the largest vessels stagger like a drunken man or tremble like an hysterical woman, under the gale and the sea, the life-boat seems at its ease, and, so to speak, at home amid the hugest waves. It is to other boats what the stormy petrel is to the different ornithological races. It must not be supposed, however, that the men who manage it do not also need great courage. As the real life-boats are most frequently required in desperate cases, the danger is nearly the same, and the circumstances in which they manœuvre are well adapted to terrify the imagination of the most intrepid men. During one of those commotions of the sea which the English call a ground-swell, the *Countess of Lisburne* fishing-boat ran upon Cardigan Bar. Her masts and sails were carried away by a gust. The waves fell one after the other upon the planks of the vessel with the dull and sepulchral sound of earth falling on a coffin.

No sooner was the danger which the barque incurred known, than the Cardigan life-boat put out to sea. The crew saw on the horizon the relics of the wreck palpitating like a living thing asking for mercy. On this day, the sea was violent enough to capsize a three-mast vessel; *à fortiori*, it sported with the frail boat as if it were an egg-shell. As the life-boat approached nearer the wreck, the waves became so terrible that it would have made the most resolute man turn pale. The unhappy men had lost their boat; and hence no hope remained to them but in the life-boat. Death staring them in the face, as the English say, they uttered piercing cries: but the crew of the life-boat had sworn to sacrifice their own lives or to save those of their brothers. They at last succeeded, against wind and sea, in reaching the three sailors comprising the crew of the *Countess of Lisburne,* and brought them safe ashore.

Men who struggle without turning pale against the sea and the unchained elements, with the noble intention of succouring their fellow-men, are naturally brave: hence the sailors and fishermen who form the life-boat crews are generally distinguished by an exemplary life. Who cannot guess the moral action exerted over such characters by the august nature of the services they are called on to perform? Has not the strength of devotion itself at times calmed and subdued in them the revolt of those passions which are the most difficult to conquer? I should be tempted to believe so after what was told me in Cornwall.

A fisherman of the name of Jim, if you like it, in his youth displayed a stern and jealous character. As he was brave, he joined the crew of one of the life-boats which protect this dangerous coast. His companions had christened him "Silent Jim." There was a very simple reason for his dark humour. Jim loved a girl loved by another fisherman, and had discovered that he was not the favourite. He conceived a cruel resentment for his rival. One evening, when the latter was expected home from fishing, Jim proceeded to the sea-shore. It was a night of thunder and lightning. Jim crept along the rocks, which he touched every now and then in order to find his road. The tempest was in the sky; a storm growled in his heart. At length he halted in a narrow path by which George, the other fisherman, must reach his cottage. All at once the sky, which was as black as a pall, was rent asunder: by the flashes of lightning Jim's practised eye discovered a boat display signals of distress. The wind had risen during the last hour, and made the waves boil like the water in a caldron. A second flash enabled Jim distinctly to recognize George's boat, which was running the greatest risk of being dashed on the reefs. He had a moment of ferocious joy; Heaven itself had undertaken to give him revenge, and all he needed to do was to leave it free to act. If it were a crime, the secret would be eternally between himself and the elements, which, to some extent, had become his accomplices. Still, his conscience told him that it was cowardly, and he became sad.

All at once he heard, through the wind and rain, voices on the beach, in the direction where was the life-boat house. He did not doubt but that the news of a boat in distress and in danger of perishing had reached the ears of his comrades. He mentally saw them leaping into the life-boat; for in such a case the brave sailors display the same eagerness in risking life as others do in preserving it. His seat would be occupied in the boat. The voice of duty and honour had spoken; he no longer hesitated, but ran to the life-boat station. When he arrived the boat was full; another man held the oar which by right belonged to him; he tore it from his hands in a sort of fury. The boat was launched, but no sign of the wreck was discovered. The boat had doubtless sunk or been broken up against the rocks. The life-boat was returning discouraged, when, by the flashes of lightning which did not cease striking the sea, as if with a red-hot sword, Jim noticed a human form appearing and disappearing on the surface of the deep. It was evidently one of the crew of the fishing-boat struggling against death. Jim seized one of the life-boat lines, leapt into the sea, and seizing the drowning man by the hair, brought him to the boat. The unhappy man was in a state of perfect insensibility; he was laid on his back, and when the life-boat reached land, attempts were made to restore him to life. On recovering, George learned by whom he had been saved. He tried to take Jim's hand, who roughly withdrew it. "Leave me alone," he said, "we shall never meet again." On the morrow he signed articles for three years on board a vessel bound for the Pacific Islands.

Respect for human life is one of the most honourable characteristics of modern civilization. Ancient societies were based on a perfectly different principle—on immolation, slavery, and war. They gloried in sacrificed victims, while in our days nations take a pride in saving them. The Life-Boat Institution marks a progress in this direction: in the sight of its members every man is worth incurring a peril to save, and this grand example has been offered by England, which has been represented so lightly by French authors as the classic country of selfishness!

Whatever may be said to the contrary, free nations are compelled to display generosity, as the duty of assisting the unfortunate is not laid as a charge on the Government: they owe it to their conscience to do good without the sanction of the State. France only possesses two or three life-boats worthy the name: she has, I am aware, on her coasts a noble population of sailors and fishermen ever ready to lend a hand; but what can devotedness effect without the mechanical means that resist the fury of a tempest? In order to build her fleet of life-boats, England appealed to everything that can raise the soul of a nation; to poetry, eloquence, and Christian faith. Has she erred in this? I do not believe it. The most religious of all societies would be the one able to say to God: "Of all those Thou hast given me, not one hath perished through my fault."

CHAPTER IX.

ANTIQUITY OF LIGHTHOUSES—WHY THEY WERE NEGLECTED IN THE MIDDLE AGES—TRINITY HOUSE—ORIGIN AND HISTORY OF THIS MARITIME INSTITUTION—CHARTER OF HENRY VIII.—TRACES OF A CATHOLIC INSTITUTION—DEPTFORD—SAYER'S COURT AND JOHN EVELYN—PETER THE GREAT—ST. NICHOLAS CHURCH AND THE DUKE OF WELLINGTON—STEPNEY AND SIR THOMAS SPERT—ELDER BROTHERS AND YOUNGER BROTHERS—HONORARY AND ACTIVE MEMBERS — DUTIES OF THE VARIOUS COMMITTEES — JAMES I. AT TRINITY HOUSE—DISASTROUS CONSEQUENCES OF ROYAL INTERFERENCE—ADVANTAGES OF THE NEW SYSTEM—THE BOARD OF TRADE—THE NORTHERN COMMISSIONERS AND THE BALLAST BOARD.

NOTHING that interests seamen is neglected by a maritime nation. England, for instance, so liberal and ingenious in saving the shipwrecked, is equally attentive in preventing shipwrecks by protecting her isles with a ball of fire. Hence a study of the lighthouses which she erects and maintains with so much zeal deserves the notice of any one who wishes not to neglect any of the characteristic aspects of English life.

Lighthouses were known in England in the most ancient times. The Normans built on the coasts of Great Britain towers which appear to have been used both as beacons and as posts of observation whence to watch the movements of hostile ships at sea. Near Dover might have been seen, a few years back, an old ruin which has since fallen down, and to which the vulgar language gave the name of the Devil's Drop of Mortar. This was the relic of an old Roman lighthouse intended to direct at night the entrance of vessels into the port. A period, however, arrived when lighting the sea-shore ceased. During the whole of the middle ages people thought much less about protecting the interests of navigation and commerce than about defending themselves against surprises and sudden attacks. Of what use would lighthouses have been then? To guide the pirates to their prey, and indicate to enemies the coasts of England. Great Britain at that time resembled the cuttle fish, which, to escape a danger, makes night around it by spreading a black liquid over the water. Prudence decreed that after sunset Albion should disappear in darkness. The narrow straits, the rocks, the shallows, the thousand perils that surround its coasts, thus formed a natural fortress which no one dared to brave. A very evident result of this system was, that in those days ships did not sail at night. Everything leads to the impression that this state of things was prolonged to the reign of Elizabeth. About the year 1600, a certain Bushell, to satisfy private demands, built two lighthouses at Caistor, which were soon followed by two others at Lowestoft. Such an innovation necessarily met with some resistance; and it is a curious fact that this resistance was chiefly offered by that maritime company which at a later date undertook the maintenance of these same ocean lamps.

At the present day there is no question as to the benefit of lighting the British coasts. There is scarcely a choice to make, according to the localities, between two quite distinct processes: the light can be fixed on a vessel or on a tower. In the first case we have what is called a lightship; in the second a lighthouse. Before examining the two methods, it will be advisable to study the administrative system presiding over the arrangement of the lights intended to indicate the line of coast or the presence of a reef. The lighthouses in Great Britain are not, as in France, in the hands of the State; some of them belong to towns or local authorities; but they are generally dependent on ancient and venerable maritime societies, which have played a great part in the political economy of the nation.

Facing the Tower of London, or rather the old moat, now converted into a charming promenade, there is a handsome grass plot all surrounded by shrubs; and behind this square rises a building which seems purposely to isolate itself from the noise and the multitude: it is Trinity House. The seat of this important maritime society was formerly in Water Lane, whence it was, so to speak, driven by two fires. Could it make a better choice than the neighbourhood of the Thames: the docks and the masts which crown it in the distance, just as parks or woods of lofty trees surround the manors of English aristocracy?

The principal features of the edifice, built in 1793, by Wyatt, consist of a massive ground floor, surmounted by a single storey, adorned with Doric columns and pilasters, all built of Portland stone. On the parade figures, which from their round plump cheeks might easily be taken for Cupids, hold in their hands anchors, compasses and sea charts: these emblems fairly indicate the character of the institution. The ground floor is occupied by the officers; the upper floor contains fine rooms, into which the public are not allowed admission, but which I was permitted to visit. A noble vestibule leads to the double stone staircase, which reunites at a central slab, decorated with ornaments and sculpture. On the right, in a semicircle formed by the wall, a large oil painting by Thomas Gainsboro's nephew is framed, representing ex-elder brethren dressed in their uniform, and forming a family party. The secretary, who has passed fifty years in the house, and has seen most of these faces closely, declares that they live again on the canvas: if you did not know them, you would wager on the likenesses. On the left are inscribed, on large glass panels, the names of benefactors of the institution, and the sums they have left it. Massive mahogany doors introduce the visitor into the board-room, the ceiling of which, painted in 1796 by Regaud, a French artist, and loaded with allegories, shows us the prosperity of England born from navigation and commerce. The British Neptune advances triumphantly, surrounded by sea-horses and attended by Tritons. In one hand he bears a trident, in the other the shield of the United Kingdom. Cannon and other warlike implements protect his march, while genii wave the standard of Great Britain. The standard may pass: but the cannon! is not this an abuse of anachronism even in painting? On the other side, Britannia, seated on a rock, is receiving the products of distant countries. Sea nymphs flock up from all parts of the world loaded with riches, and sailors spread these fruits of commerce along the shores of England. Infants are shaking torches representing the lighthouses that surround the British coasts, and direct during the night the movements of vessels. The walls of this room are decorated with full-length portraits of George III. and William IV. and their consorts, for royalty itself has figured in the annals of Trinity House, and sovereigns honour themselves by wearing the insignia of the brotherhood, of which they have been brethren or patrons. The portrait of the Duke of Wellington, by Lucas, is considered the best existing of the victor of Waterloo. The busts of Queen Victoria and Prince Albert, sculptured in white marble, by Noble, one of the few living sculptors who have attained celebrity in England, solemnly repose at either side of the mantel-piece. Twenty easy chairs, arranged round a vast semicircular table covered with green baize, mark the places of the members of the Council at their meetings.

The members of Trinity House thought, with Ben Jonson, that good meals keep up fraternity. Their dining-room, lighted by a sort of round lantern in the ceiling, displays what might be called a tranquil and substantial luxury. I noticed there the bust of Pitt, by Chantrey, portraits of the Earl of Sandwich, the Duke of Bedford, Sir Francis Drake, and more especially that of Kenelm Digby, by Vandyck. Here was recently given a grand banquet in honour of the Prince of Wales. At regular distances, excellent models of lighthouses, kept under glass cases, remind one of the serious object of this society, which was founded by Henry VIII.

The history of the Trinity House is not at all known to the English themselves: a portion of its old archives was destroyed by fire in 1714, and perhaps, like all ancient corporations, it was not very anxious to communicate to the profane the mysteries of its annals.* All that is known is, that it exists by virtue of a charter of Henry VIII., dated at Canterbury, March 20th, 1512, and not, as has been hitherto believed, at Westminster, May 20th, 1514. The original of this deed has been lost; but if such a document, of which an authentic copy is in existence, could be found, it would throw no light on the real age of the society. Is the date of the deed of incorporation really that of its origin? There is reason for doubting it. Most of these old associations arose from a community of interests and business. Men attached to each other by the tie of the same trade generally combined to establish certain rules, and take certain measures from which they would derive advantage. At a later date, when they had acquired influence, and the utility of their services was generally recognized, they applied to the State to obtain a licence. The royal charter, consequently, only recognized and consecrated acquired rights, while adding to them certain privileges. We may fairly believe that the brotherhood of sailors existed long before it was recognized by the authorities; perhaps it even dates back to the cradle of British navigation; but why the name of Trinity House? Is it because the first brethren met on certain days in a chapel consecrated to the Trinity? Is it be-

* It is through the extreme kindness of Mr. Berthon, the secretary, that I possess information hitherto neglected.

cause Henry VIII. instituted at the same time three societies of sailors, those at Deptford, Newcastle, and Hull? The field remains open for conjectures; but the most accredited opinion is that this corporation was called Trinity Board, or Trinity House, from the terms of Henry VIII.'s charter beginning with the words: "In the name of the most glorious and indivisible Trinity." At a later date, in another deed, the Prince added to it an invocation to St. Clement, and the latter name was frequently used to designate the corporation or guild.

We must not lose sight of the fact that this brotherhood was originally founded under the inspiration of religious ideas, or perhaps even monastic ones. The duty of the members of the association was to pray for the souls of sailors drowned at sea, and for the lives of those who struggled against the tempests. Henry VIII., at the beginning, retained this character, and even forced the brothers and sisters to perform certain devotional practices. A chaplain must be elected and paid by the association to celebrate masses. In the second half of the reign of Henry VIII., the reformatory movement soon effaced what were already called relics of Papistry. Of the religious feeling which presided over its birth, the fraternity of sailors only retained charity; it founded a school for children, and an almshouse for old indigent sailors. Thus modified by Protestantism, this old Catholic association freed itself from the forms of the middle ages, and separated the civil from the mystical element. What was the object of the society? To increase the knowledge of the sailors and develop the navigation of the kingdom.

The seat of this brotherhood was originally at Deptford, an old fishing village situated in a deep creek formed by the Thames in the vicinity of London. Judging the position favourable, Henry VIII. made a dock there in 1513, and built an arsenal. This dock soon became one of the most important in the kingdom. During his stay in England, Peter the Great visited it in order to study the ship-building art. He lodged then in the house of John Evelyn. Sayer's Court was at that time the favourite meeting-place of celebrated authors, learned men, and persons of taste. Not satisfied with steering a yacht on the Thames every day, and working in the dockyards, the Czar of all the Russias was fond of being wheeled in a barrow through the walks of the celebrated gardens that surrounded Sayer's Court. He managed so well that he destroyed all the hedges, excepting those of holly, which, says Evelyn, had means to defend themselves; *illum nemo imprime lacessit*. These gardens have entirely disappeared, and the victualling yard now stands on their site.

I sought a long time in Deptford for traces

of the old associations whence the Trinity House issued. An old mansion in which the brethren held their meetings was pulled down in 1787: it was in this house that the byelaws of the institution were drawn up. And doubtless in memory of the cradle of the fraternity, the members of Trinity House still proceed to Deptford or its neighbourhood to celebrate certain solemnities. Two almshouses attached to the institution still exist: one dates from the reign of Henry VIII., though rebuilt in 1788; the other was built toward the end of the last century. St. Nicholas Church has also possibly something to tell us about the origin of the brotherhood. In this church, which doubtless served as a nucleus of the association, the principal members of the brotherhood assembled on Trinity Monday, up to within a few years; and the inhabitants of Deptford remember having seen the Duke of Wellington enter the church as a member of Trinity House.

Close to Deptford, but on the other side of the Thames, is the old village of Stepney, now a suburb of London. In Stepney Church is a monument on which the following inscription can be read:—" Sir Thomas Spert, for some time Controller of the Navy to Henry VIII., founder and first master of the worthy corporation called Trinity House." This monument was erected by the said corporation in 1622, or eighty-one years after the death of the man whose memory they wished to honour. This Sir Thomas Spert was a great favourite of Henry VIII., and it was by his advice that the King founded or rather established the Trinity House.

Queen Elizabeth confirmed the existence of this maritime society by an Act of Parliament. Charters were afterwards granted to it by James I., Charles II., and James II. I saw these venerable deeds in the office religiously kept in an old box of black shagreen. What was the object of the author of these new charters? To explain the liberties, franchises, and privileges of the society, which had been rather vaguely indicated by Henry VIII. Far from extending the jurisdiction of the brotherhood, all that was done was to place restrictions upon it. Is not the defining of a power the limiting of it? The society must in the first place exercise a surveillance, not only over the mercantile marine, but also over the State navy. This latter privilege was withdrawn in the reign of Henry VIII., when that king appointed commissioners to inspect the vessels of war. Trinity House, however, retained during this reign, and even in the following reigns, some branches of the maritime police, which gradually passed into other hands. Its constitution was also remodelled several times.

The society at the present day is divided into elder and younger brothers. This distinction did not exist at the commencement. According to the deed of foundation, the sailors of England were called on to join this society: all were represented in it, and helped in passing the laws. The charter of Henry VIII. was therefore, as we should say now-a-days, entirely democratic; those that followed it gradually effaced this character. This distinction between the elder and younger brethren was introduced in the reign of James I. That king authorized the master, directors, and assistants of Trinity House to choose from the association of sailors eighteen persons who would henceforth bear the title of elder brothers. This was the source of the present management. The same charter for the first time prohibited the younger brothers from voting the laws and regulations relating to the affairs of the company: it however allowed them the right of taking part in the deliberations whenever the master and directors were about to be elected or removed. At a later date the charters of Charles II. and James II. only left them the right of nominating, but not that of removing, the members of the Council. Those who attended the elections received for their trouble half-a-crown instead of a dinner. In the course of time this privilege, the right of electing, was taken from them. The pretext employed to exclude the younger brothers from a share in the vote and the affairs of the society was, that they were too noisy at the meetings. At the present day the younger brothers are elected by the good pleasure of the Council, on the proposition of one of the elder brothers, and their election is not submitted to a vote, as was formerly the case.

The ceremony of reception took place at Deptford on Trinity Monday, according to an old custom kept up till 1709. This ceremony, which was very simple, consisted in the new member taking the oath, and then shaking the hand of each elder brother, who bade him welcome in return. This done, he received a branch, the name given to a certificate bearing the signature of the society. He then had to pay twenty shillings for the poor, as entrance fee. The number of younger brothers is unlimited; it could not be too great, the old charters say, because sailors represent the strength of the nation. In our time, however, they only amount to 360. Must we not regret that Trinity House has, during the course of time, introduced into its constitution far too much of the thoroughly British principle of primogeniture? The elders have seized on the power, honour, and profits of the institution, while they have left the younger an empty name and a dry branch. The same thing has happened here as occurs but too often in English families.

The elder brothers, thirty-one in number, must be elected from among the younger brothers.

By virtue of this principle, whenever the society wished to elect a great man, he was first received as a younger brother, and then (very often on the same day) raised to the dignity of an elder brother. The younger brothers are, consequently, candidates for the higher rank of the fraternity; but in Trinity House, as in the kingdom of Heaven, there are more called than are chosen, and the majority of them remain in the state of perpetual candidates. By a modification of the rules, made in 1835, every younger brother who aspires to promotion must undergo a sort of examination into the validity of his title. No one is allowed to present himself unless he has previously served at least four years as a captain in the navy or the mercantile marine. On election day, a list of the approved candidates is handed by the secretary to all the members of the court present. Each of them, beginning with the youngest, marks with a scratch of a pen the names of three who appear to him eligible. This done, the names of those three who have received the most ticks are put up to ballot, and the one who receives most balls is proclaimed duly elected. The new elder brother pays £30 for the poor, and the same sum for a dinner. At one of the next meetings he takes the oath, and henceforth forms part of the Trinity House board.

The elder brothers are divided into honorary and active members. From the earlier times the company has understood the benefit of receiving into its ranks men unacquainted with navigation, but celebrated through their birth, social position, or great services rendered to the country. In 1673, a Bishop of Rochester, who preached before the corporation on Trinity Monday, was elected a brother. Pitt held the dignity of Master for seventeen years. George IV. was performing the same duties when he ascended the throne. Lord Palmerston has taken the place of Prince Albert and Wellington. Around him are grouped statesmen holding very different views —Earl Russell, for instance, and Lord Derby: a rhetorical figure dear to the English language— the vessel of the State—is the only bond attaching them to a maritime association. These honorary members, eleven in number, have no salary; they do not at all interfere with the internal affairs of the house, but invest it with brilliancy and influence. In the case of decease, their seats are filled up by a majority of votes, and their successor is sought in the same exalted sphere of government or national glory. The twenty active members, to whom the material interests of the company are in reality intrusted, are old captains of ships of the line or merchant vessels, who have retired from the service.

The effective council of Trinity House is composed of a deputy master, of four masters, of eight assistants, and seven other elder brethren.

These twenty members are divided into six committees, which manage all the affairs of the corporation. The first, called the Committee of Wardens, is composed of the deputy master and masters; it occupies itself more especially with the finances, and exerts a control over the whole of the society's operations. The five other committees, according to the various duties assigned to them, appoint pilots and give them certificates of efficiency, watch the ballasting of ships in the Thames, establish or keep up all the sea marks, examine the pupils of Christ's Hospital who are intended for the sea, collect the revenues of the society, or else look after the boarders in the houses of refuge belonging to Trinity House. The charters also confer on them the right of punishing sailors for mutiny, bad conduct, or desertion. The navy, as well as the mercantile marine, is probably of all professions the one which in Great Britain offers the best prospects for personal merit. Several of the officers who have risen to the highest rank in the service of the State commenced by climbing the mast, and Captain Cook himself started as cabin boy in a collier. Among the old captains who direct Trinity House, there are several who can call themselves the sons of their works; they are practical men, in whom naval experience is allied with the energetic resolution to protect the interests of commerce.

THE RIGHT OF ERECTING LIGHTHOUSES. 241

Among the varied and extensive duties of this society, I will only dwell on those that concern the lighting of the British seas. In the reign of James I., it was asked for the first time whether the privileges granted to Trinity House by Henry VIII. and Queen Elizabeth embraced the right of erecting lighthouses. One person was specially interested in proving the contrary opinion this was the King. The granting of lighthouses was a source of favour, and consequently a thing that might be counted on to extend the prerogative of the Crown. So thought James I., and the courtiers were of his opinion. At that time there was not a bare and desolate rock on the sea-shore which was not coveted by speculators to build a tower on and light a beacon. An ex-Minister of State, who stood very well at Court, Lord Grenville, wrote in his journal, in the shape of a note or memorandum, " Watch the moment when the King is in good temper to ask him for a lighthouse." These lighthouses, in fact, raised considerable dues from all the ships that passed within the light thrown by the lanterns. The claims of James I. greatly embarrassed the judges, who eventually effected a compromise between the two parties; it was decided that the brotherhood of sailors had a right to erect lighthouses, but that the Crown enjoys the same privilege by virtue of the common law.

From this moment the monopoly of the

beacons lighted on the coasts, instead of remaining the exclusive property of Trinity House, as Elizabeth wished, was granted or sold by the Sovereign to private persons. The consequences of this system were deplorable. Some of the beacons gave a bad light; others were not lit at all; and in all cases the ships had heavy dues to pay. At length, in the reign of William IV., an Act of Parliament introduced a species of uniformity into the administration of the lighthouses, and reduced the tolls. This act decided that all the interests of the Sovereign in the lighthouse question should pass into the hands of Trinity House for a sum of £300,000, paid once for all to the commissioners of the Crown. It also authorized the board to buy lighthouses belonging to private persons, and in case of dispute, the value must be decided by a jury. It was at this moment that the abuses of the old system became visible to the country. One of the proprietors did not blush to ask for a sterile rock, situated in the middle of the ocean, and with a house on it, the enormous sum of £550,000; he ended by accepting with a sigh £400,000. The source of these immense profits evidently lay in the tolls raised on navigation. The lighthouses belonging to individuals charged ships at that date twopence per ton.

Since the same lighthouses have belonged to Trinity House, the tolls vary between half a farthing and a penny; and yet the cost of lighting, and consequently the volume of light, have greatly increased under the new management. The lighthouse of Small's Rock, above the Bristol Channel, only used 200 gallons of oil a year when it was in private hands; it now consumes 1,500 gallons. We can see by this what services Trinity House has rendered to navigation under this head. The collection of the tolls, nevertheless, constitutes a very important part of its revenue; it is with this money, as well as the sale of ballast for ships, and the produce of its estates—partly purchased, partly inherited—that the society covers all its expenses. One of the principal charges is the construction and maintenance of lighthouses and other signal marks which warn ships at sea. It also devotes a great part of its funds to works of charity; and for this reason it has been exempted, like the English hospitals, from the public taxes. Trinity House constitutes a connecting link between the Admiralty and the mercantile marine. Independent of the State, but drawing to it the celebrated and influential members of the Government, supported too by charters which secure it a legitimate and tolerably exclusive authority, it is the type of those truly English institutions in which power, as it were, offers a hand to liberty.

What Trinity House is to England—a brotherhood of sailors directing the police and navigation of the seas, the Northern Commissioners and the Ballast Board are to Scotland and Ireland. These three societies were placed, in 1853, under the control of the Board of Trade, whose offices are in the Treasury. The latter is a branch of the Government — a Committee of the Privy Council, having at its head a president, vice-president, and two secretaries. Its duties are rather extensive. The different laws relating to the interests of commerce, treaties and negotiations concerning trade, changes in the management and balance of the customs, are generally discussed in its offices. The woods and forests also fall under its jurisdiction.

It is easy to discern the intention of the Government in attaching the three great maritime corporations of the kingdom to the Board of Trade: it was desired to give them a character of unity. But we must not apply our French ideas to the system of British institutions. With us, a central power is *de facto* an absorbing power; it directs, it regulates, it orders, it takes from individual liberty all it can without standing in too flagrant contradiction with the law. Such is not at all the character of State intervention among our neighbours. The Board of Trade has no influence over the affairs of Trinity House except in money details.

It is certainly a great thing to hold the purse strings, and in financial questions the ¦Board of Trade exerts a direct influence over the administration of the society. Do you wish for an instance? Prior to 1854, if it was desired to build a lighthouse in some locality near the sea, the merchants and shipowners interested in the success of the enterprise drew up petitions, begging Trinity House to light such and such dangerous point on the coast. They also pledged themselves to pay a fair toll to the company, in order to cover its expenses. If the utility of the light was proved to it, the corporation applied to the Crown for a licence bearing the Royal Seal, authorizing it to raise the agreed-on toll upon passing vessels. At the present day, the Board of Trade, before allowing the funds of the company to be ventured in building a lighthouse, generally itself examines whether the measure is needed. However this may be, this State surveillance has rendered the old motto of the society more true: *Trinitas in unitate.*

Among the several processes which help to light the British seas, there is one that thoroughly belongs to England, and to which the name of floating lights is given; it is this we will now proceed to examine.

CHAPTER X.

FLOATING LIGHTS—THE NORE LIGHT—ROBERT HAMBLIN—GEOLOGICAL LAW DETERMINING THE EXISTENCE OF LIGHT-VESSELS—THE GOODWIN SANDS—THE SCILLY ISLES—SCIENCE AND LEGENDS—THE 'MAIDEN BOWER'—AN OFFICIOUS CICERONE—GENERAL APPEARANCE OF THE ISLES—ST. MARY'S AND HUGH TOWN—MY LANDLORD'S HOUSE—TWO ROMANTIC SISTERS—SUNDAY AT ST. MARY'S—MANNERS OF THE INHABITANTS—MATERNITY BEFORE MARRIAGE — THE DOCTOR, POLICEMAN, AND GARRISON — THE CASSITERIDES OF THE GREEKS—MR. UGUSTUS SMITH—CELTIC ANTIQUITIES — TRADE OF THE SCILLY MEN — AGRICULTURE, GARDENS AND FARMS — THE ISLAND FLORA — THE BUILDING MANIA.

TRAVELLERS going from France to England by steamer will have noticed during the night, at the mouth of the Thames, a light which guides all the ships of the world to the port of London. This light, called the Nore Light, was placed on a beacon vessel to indicate a perfidious sandbank, the Nore sand.

The inventor of this system of lighting was a certain Robert Hamblin, who lived in the last century. Formerly a barber at Lynn, he married in that town the daughter of a captain, and possibly on account of this alliance fancied himself a bit of a sailor. The fact is, that though not bred to the sea, he became master of a coasting collier. This trade does not appear to have enriched him; and after failing in several enterprises, he resolved to introduce a new system for distinguishing naval lights from each other. Chance brought him into contact with a man of great plans, David Avery, who woke up every morning with his head full of millions and with empty pockets. Acting in concert, they obtained from the English Government a patent for fourteen years to work their invention.

Passing soon from one plan to another, they established at the Nore a floating light on board a vessel, and then took it on themselves to raise tolls, intended to maintain the light. This latter part appeared to the Trinity House an infraction of its privileges. The light-vessel had proved a success, and was highly approved by seafaring men. Encouraged by this success, David Avery, who appears to have played the principal part in the execution of the project, openly announced his intention of establishing a similar vessel off the Scilly Islands. The moment seemed at hand when all Britain would be surrounded by a belt of floating lights. The members of Trinity House, in their quality of guardians of the navigation, complained to the Lords of the Admiralty, who could not or would not act. The Maritime Society then addressed the King, and represented to him how illegal it was for an individual to lay a toll on the mercantile marine. It managed so cleverly that the patent was quashed on May 4th, 1732. Avery, whose chance of a fortune was overthrown by this thunderbolt, went to the company, and proposed to treat with it about the Nore Light. He asserted that he had spent £2,000. They capitulated the patent, and the ownership of the lightboat passed over in perpetuity to Trinity House; but Avery was granted a lease of it for sixty-one years on the payment of £100 annually. Such is the origin of the floating lights. Hamblin and Avery have not an odour of sanctity with the members of the Trinity Board; still, I see no reason for treating them with disdain; the invention was useful, and the proof is that it has survived. It is true it has been asserted that the same idea had been proposed fifty years previously by Sir John Clayton. The Trinity House declined the proposal, while the two adventurers, if they should be called so, had at least the honour and merit of carrying it out.

Lighting the seas by vessels is subject to certain geological conditions. There are now forty-one floating lights in England, while there are five in Ireland, and only one in Scotland. Must not there be a reason for this, or, as naturalists say, a geographical law determining the distribution of light-vessels on the surface of the ocean? The law is as follows: the coasts of Scotland and Ireland are principally composed of granite and porphyry: disintegrated for centuries, these masses have formed at certain spots accumulations of sandbanks, producing straits very dangerous of access; but still solid blocks remain on which lighthouses can be built. It is not precisely the same in the south and east of England: there nearly the whole line of seaboard consists of cliffs of chalk and other friable rocks, while the bottom of the sea is a bed of sand: under such circumstances, where can a base be found sufficiently firm to lay the foundations of a tower destined to brave the wind, the tempests, and sometimes even the assaults of the waves? It is at such localities that the light-vessels render special services.

One of the spots most feared by sailors is on the Kent coast, what are called the Goodwin Sands, which, if we may believe certain stories, possess the property of devouring ships. Various attempts to build a lighthouse on them having failed, these floating lights have been established on this sinister bank, which warn vessels, and have certainly prevented several wrecks. Similar signals are employed at Yarmouth, in the Lowestoft Roads, and elsewhere, for mostly the same causes. Lastly the lightship, in other and very different localities, is used to guard sailors against treacherous currents, subterranean whirlpools, or reefs cunningly hidden at certain hours by the high tide. The floating light of the Scilly Islands is specially intended for this purpose.

Curious to visit this light-vessel, situated at the south-western extremity of England, I went on board at Penzance in 1863. What I had read about the Scilly Islands gave me the idea of scattered isles and rocks, inhabited for the most part by seals and savages. Thirty-six miles of sea separate Penzance from St. Mary's, the place where I intended first to stop. On deck, a tall active man, wearing a cap, and with a foot as firm as a sailor's, walked up and down with extraordinary agility, in spite of the rolling and heaving of the steamer. He seemed to know everybody, even those persons he had never seen before. Having doubtless guessed my weak point, he pointed out to me and mentioned all the curious places on the coast. Thanks to this obliging cicerone I was able to salute in passing Treryn Castle, a formidable promontory crowned with a moving rock (the Logan Stone); the Runnel, a dark reef covered at high water; the granitic masses of Pensorth, one of the imposing features of the coast; and lastly, Land's End, which rose sad and haughty at a distance of two or three miles. There are certain beauties in nature, like certain events in history, which appear grander at a distance.

Ere long we lost sight of land, and found ourselves between water and sky. If tradition may be credited, there was a time when this solution of continuity did not exist: a slip of land extended between what is now the Land's End and the Scilly Isles. There were, it is asserted, green and fertile plains, studded with villages and the steeples of 140 churches. The country was called at that time Lethowson, or Lyonnesse: this is the name still given to the arm of the sea which separates the extremity of Cornwall from the Scilly Isles. According to the old romances, the land of Lyonnesse was the scene of a sanguinary battle. There " during the whole day the noise of fighting rolled among the mountains and along the sea-shore, until all the Knights of the Round Table had fallen round their King Arthur."

Where is this land of beauty now, and how did it disappear? It is at the bottom of the sea. Vague stories told by fishermen state that relics of doors and windows, fragments of mill-stones, and other vestiges, have now and then been drawn up in the nets. An old country family, the Trevelyans, bear in their arms a horse issuing from the sea, in memory of one of their ancestors, who during the inundation succeeded in reaching the Cornish coast on the back of his charger, which was an intrepid swimmer. Why must these fables be contradicted on the authority of Strabo, who describes the spot much as it is now? Geology, however, has no grounds for rejecting the base of the legend, especially since Lyell's theories have called attention to the last encroachments of the sea. These waters are sufficiently deep and tempestuous to have forced an ancient barrier. Some isolated rocks, such as the Wolf and the Seven Stones, certainly seem to be the relics of an isthmus which, shaken by subterranean convulsions, or gradually undermined by the waves, one day fell violently into the Atlantic; but a sort of cloud or impenetrable veil covers the date of the event.

After two or three hours at sea we perceived on the horizon what looked like a group of petrified clouds: it was the Scilly Isles. My cicerone then told me that he was an inhabitant of St. Mary's, and could accommodate me with a lodging in his house. I am not fond of inns: hotels are in travelling what commonplace remarks are in conversation: hence I gladly accepted his proposal, and we made our arrangements accordingly. I did not the less admire his cleverness, and began to modify slightly my first opinion as to the simplicity of the Scillonians. *En route* we passed a pretty vessel, *The Maiden Bower*, all covered with flags, which had been launched that morning, and which we undertook to tow back to port. The two crews exchanged loud huzzas, hats were waved thrice in the air, and I understood that it was a manner of saluting the new comer on the sea, by wishing it every sort of prosperity. My host (for I already considered him such) told me that *The Maiden Bower* had been built at the islands; these savages consequently possessed at least excellent notions about naval architecture!

For some time we coasted frowning rocks, prodigious natural fortresses. The first sight of these islands is most singular: if ever our continents are swallowed up by the sea they will have this form. Scattered and torn strips of granite seem to float on the surface of a sea full of terror and grandeur. At the first sight these islets appeared uninhabited; they might be called the ruins of a world. A vast ocean, on which the sunbeams were beginning to decline, roared with an imperious air around this truly wrecked land, which was, however, protected by a bristling belt of cliffs.

It was about six in the evening when we entered Port St. Mary's, which is surrounded by a long curvilinear pier, built between 1835 and 1838. The quay was covered with people, who had flocked up, I imagine, to welcome the entrance of the new vessel. What was my amazement at finding all the fashions of London! The women wore round straw hats, and spoke English with an accent much purer than the Cornish. We entered the town, or, as it is called, the capital of the island, Hugh Town, by a narrow and rather dark passage, like that of a fortress. We passed through neatly-built streets and a square called the Parade, on which an interpreter, recognizing a Frenchman in me, came to offer his services. He is a Spaniard by birth, who speaks all languages without knowing one. An elegant shop attracted my attention: I entered; and after I had been served, the tradesman gave me my copper change in a small bag, with all the politeness of the West End. I had decidedly deceived myself as to the manners of the Scillonians.

My host's house was built of granite, like most of the houses in Hugh Town. He was married to an Irishwoman, who did not regret her country. As both were obliged to go out to lay in a stock of provisions, they left me master of the house. It was a Saturday, the visiting day, and they begged me to receive the visitors. I cannot say that they intrusted to me the keys of the house, for there were none; the rooms, drawers, and wardrobes were all open, with the good faith of the primitive ages. I was scarce alone ere I heard a knock at the street door. I rose to open it, when two sisters deliberately entered the kitchen. They were the daughters of a farmer of the island, but there was nothing rustic in their dress or manners. The elder, tall, strong, and high-coloured, was learned; she had acquired mathematics, history, and French at Hugh Town: she was engaged to a young man of St. Mary's, and wore on her finger a gold ring of betrothal. The other was about eighteen years of age, with more delicate features, and an air of natural distinction. Neither of them had as yet left the island, and yet they were possessed by a desire of knowing the world. They spoke of Penzance as Virgil's shepherds speak of the great city—"*Urbem quam dicunt Romam;*" and their father had promised to take them next year to the mainland, if they were very good.

At Hugh Town, the only guide one has at night is the moon and the stars, which do not shine at all during the winter. What a great marvel a town lighted with gas seemed to them! Neither had any idea of what a theatre was like, though the elder had read all Shakspeare's plays. The king must be very handsome on the stage, if his costume resembled the descriptions and engravings; but it was the princess that they most desired to see. This mixture of intellectual culture and ignorance of society had something interesting about it. They were very fond of romances, and if they had felt their wings at liberty, I believe that the sea would not have held them back. "Who knows," the younger exclaimed, "what might happen to us in foreign countries?" and by foreign countries she evidently meant England. While talking, the two sisters bravely set about getting supper ready, which had hitherto been cooking all alone on the hob, as if it were accustomed to manage itself. They, however, considered it useful to blow up the fire with a Cyclopean pair of bellows, a massive relic of the primitive days of civilization.

A second knock was dealt the door; it was their father come to join them. Dressed in good black cloth, this visitor looked thoroughly respectable, as the English say. He was proud of his daughters; and as the extent of their acquirements was represented in his mind by the sum of money he had paid for their instruction, he liked repeating that he had spent £60 on their education. During this time my hosts returned. The supper consisted of an enormous lobster, caught that morning in the bay. We did not separate till eleven o'clock; and, as I was still under the impression of the steamboat, I felt myself at sea the whole night. The same breeze I had heard whistling in my ears during the day, the same waves which had raged round the ship, seemed to whistle and rage against my windows, for the sea was so close to them. St. Mary's, the largest of the Scilly Isles, is only eight or nine miles in circumference, and Hugh Town is built on a narrow strip of land jutting out into the sea. This position is charming but dangerous; and the prophets of evil have predicted that Hugh Town, some day or another, will be carried away by a deluge.

I was awakened on Sunday morning by the sound of psalms, which reached me from an adjoining chapel. St. Mary's possesses two churches, the old and the new. The old church stands in the middle of the fields; it is a venerable ruin, in which the burial service is still read now and then. The new church is a rather large building, erected in 1837, the principal ornament of which is simplicity. The religious movement is besides dominated by dissenting sects, and the Ranters have lately produced a real reformation in the morals of the inhabitants. There are two schools in the town, one for boys and girls, the other, more advanced, for adults. In winter public lectures are given at night by grown-up persons in the children's school.

A feature worthy of notice in honour of the population of St. Mary's is, that in this island there are no poor. If any islander is incapable of gaining his livelihood, others come to his aid without saying a word, so that you never meet in town or country misery in rags. Drunkenness is unknown there, especially among the women. The girls have an independent character, and do not like to go into service. They might possibly engage themselves in foreign families; but in the island, where all know each other, and live on a certain footing of equality, their pride would suffer in obeying a mistress. They generally learn a trade, such as dressmaking or millinery. The lads, for their part, study navigation at school, and become something better than common sailors. The young men nearly always marry girls of the island; but it is not rare for them to court for eight or ten years before tying the irrevocable knot. I am obliged to add that there is a secret reason for this long patience.

Marriage here is nearly always a consequence of maternity: it is not maternity which, as elsewhere, is the fruit of marriage. A Protestant clergyman, who lived on the island for fourteen years, only saw in that whole time two first-born children come into the world more than nine months after the ceremony. He was so delighted at this uncommon occurrence, that he gave one of the mothers a pretty cap for her child, and the other a gilt-edged Bible.

There is only one doctor for all the islands; hence he is fetched in a boat, and taken four or six miles by sea to the villages scattered behind formidable cliffs. When two women are confined at the same time, one of them must do without the aid of science, unless the child is good enough to await the doctor's return. This physician, who is a great favourite, on account of his disinterestedness and benevolence, carries on his functions amid wind and tide. Public force is represented at St. Mary's by a policeman, a carpenter by trade, who works by day, but at night assumes the official garb, and walks majestically about the port. The island is also defended by a citadel, known by the name of Star Castle. This citadel or fort touches Hugh Town. You reach it by climbing up a steep hill, rising about 160 feet above the level of the sea; and before the gate is hung a bell, intended to be rung in case of alarm. Star Castle was built in 1593, during the reign of Elizabeth: it contains rather extensive buildings, quarters for the officers, a powder magazine, and barracks, and is protected by batteries, the principal of which, armed with four guns, rises on the side of Morning Point. The ramparts now form a pleasant promenade, the fine sand of which, sparkling with grains of mica, is covered with gorse bushes and gigantic shrubs. At the entrance I met a tall sergeant, who appeared to me the master of the place. I asked him how many men he had under his orders. "At this moment," he answered, "I am the garrison; but the fort has lodged in my time ten soldiers; and as there is some talk of a general war, I hope that we shall be placed on a footing of war again." In the meanwhile he was assisted in his military duties by his wife, who held the keys of the fort.

These islands are the Cassiterides, or ten islands of the Greeks; but hardly any traces of extensive mines are found on them. It is probable that the ancients confounded this archipelago with the Cornish coast, as regards the production of metal. The Romans converted it into a place of banishment. Antonius is the first who describes it by the name of *Sillariæ insulæ*, which appears to be derived from the Breton word *Sullèh*, "rocks dedicated to the sun."* These islands were conquered

* According to others, the name is derived from *Silya*, a salt-water eel, owing to the trade the old inhabitants carried on in

by Athelstan, the first Saxon king, who subjected the Cornish Britons about the year 938. During the civil wars between Charles I. and the Parliament, they at first held by the King; but they were reduced, in 1651, by Admiral Blake and Sir George Eysem. On the coast of Trescau Isle stands a gloomy tower, which still bears the name of Cromwell's Castle, and nearly facing the tower is a rock called Hangman's Isle, because, according to tradition, some mutinous soldiers were hung at this spot by the Republican troops.

The Scilly Isles formerly belonged to the Crown: they passed—it is not exactly known how—to the Duchy of Cornwall; but since the reign of Elizabeth, they have been let to private persons for a limited period. The lessee of these isles at present is Mr. Augustus Smith, who lives on Trescau Island, nearly facing St. Mary's. Mr. Smith's manor-house consists of a number of modern buildings, hanging in a very picturesque manner on the front of a rock. Who would expect to find at the foot of these arid cliffs two fresh-water lakes, extending through a delightful and well-cultivated valley? Mr. Smith has laid out gardens on the ruins of an old abbey, founded in the tenth century, and the creeping plants which have invaded the columns and windows

---

this fish. The bay to the north of St. Agnes is still called Perconger. Scilly Isle, which has given its name to the group, is a massive rock separated in two by a yawning abyss.

cover, without hiding them, all the delicate architectural lines. The rarest flowers grow profusely on the gnarled surface of the granite rocks: geraniums rise several feet above the head of the walkers; all the wealth of exotic vegetation is pompously displayed in the open air. In spite of the winds the climate of these isles is very mild, and in sheltered spots tropical plants succeed admirably. The lord of the manor had, some years ago, the idea of acclimatizing ostriches on Trescau. He began with four of these birds, which have since increased and multiplied. Mr. Augustus Smith is a sort of viceroy, whose somewhat dictatorial authority extends over the whole group of the Scilly Isles. Only five of them— St. Mary's, Trescau, St. Martin's, St. Agnes, and Brehar—are inhabited. The others, about 140 in number, are only islets covered with a scanty grass crop, and frequented by maritime birds.

St. Agnes boasts a church, one or two shops, and a fine lighthouse. One of the islands now uninhabited, Sampson, had till recently three houses and three families; but the parents died, and the children, fired by ambition, have deserted their humble natal soil. St. Helen's Isle, where the ruins of a church may be seen, is now merely occupied by a herd of deer and a few goats, which have grown wild again. When a stranger visits their domain these animals watch him anxiously, and fly to the top of the rocks; they only reassume an air of assurance when they see the intruder going away in his boat. In another islet live two donkeys, that salute with a melancholy braying the passage of boats, as if to show that they have not yet lost a feeling for society. These donkeys formerly inhabited St. Mary's, where they were accused of destroying the hedges, and doubtless of committing other damage. They were consequently tried and transported, by Mr. Smith's orders, to this desert rock. The fishermen as they pass give them bits of ship biscuit, which the poor exiles eat with a look of gratitude.

The Scilly Isles offer a great interest as regards Celtic antiquities. Borlase, an historian and antiquary, asserts that the ancient Druids honoured in rocks one of the personifications of Deity. Could they select anything better for this than a sea studded with islands, whose abrupt flanks, lashed by the furious waves, rise on all sides with a stern and desolate grandeur? I do not believe there is a spot in the world where the granite has assumed stranger, more solemn, and more religious shapes, in the sense in which the old adorers of nature understood it. These grey and solemn masses, these heaps of stones thrown up in a sublime disorder, like the convulsed cities of the giants, this moaning of the sea, repeated by the echoes of the caverns, all announce that such coasts must formerly have served as sacred places. These rocks have received strange names, according to the resemblance they are supposed to bear to works of human art or industry. The Druid's Chair, for instance, is a massive easy chair of granite, in which it is pleasant to believe that the high-priest sat to contemplate the sunrise.

Borlase is also of opinion that some of the rocks were artificially chiselled, in order to form gutters and rock basins, intended to collect the rain water used in lustral ceremonies. Geologists have since proved that the mere force of the elements may have produced such traces by decomposing the texture of the granite. These cups of natural water have not the less a singular character, and, attracted by the hoarse cry of the gulls, I stopped several times before the hard rocks which are kind enough to supply the birds with water.

One of the curiosities which have most occupied antiquaries is the Logan Rocks, a few specimens of which is found at St. Mary's. The Scilly Isles also contain several barrows; and in a cairn on Sampson, opened a few years ago by Mr. Smith's orders, a granite coffin and some bones were found. At St. Mary's, near a tower called the Telegraph, and from the top of which the coast-guardsmen observe everything that goes on around, I visited an ancient cromlech, half hidden by brambles, which has received the name of the Giant's Cave. This monument consists of three blocks of granite, lying on lateral stones that support them, and these form towards the centre a species of cavity, through which a man can pass by crawling.

There is also on the island a curious specimen of what the English call cliff-castles. On the faith of the name, however, you must not expect to find a citadel built in accordance with the modern art of our engineers: these castles, on the contrary, announce the absence of all architecture. Borlase attributes to the Danes the traces of clumsy military works which are discovered round one of the cliffs of St. Mary's; but the vulgar, who are fond of the marvellous, have given it the name of the Giant's Castle. It is not merely on the stones and monuments of nature that the ancient Britons have engraved traces of their passage; some Celtic customs have been preserved in the memories of the inhabitants. At midsummer, the Cornish coast facing the Scilly Isles is crowned with bonfires. All the antiquaries attribute the origin of this custom to the ancient Druids, who believed that they thus attracted the blessing of Heaven on the fruits of the earth which were beginning to ripen.

It is difficult not to be struck by the resemblance which must have existed formerly between this part of England and French Brittany. It was the same race of inhabitants, the same language, almost the same configuration of the rocks. At the present day the difference is great. While unalterable dogmas, feudal traditions, and the customs of the old regime kept our Britons in ignorance and misery, the Celts, on the other side of the Channel, found in religious and political liberty means of overcoming the ungrateful conditions nature had imposed upon them.

The inhabitants of the Scilly Isles are very industrious; some are pilots, others ship-builders or farmers. The interior of St. Mary's is a delicious garden, surrounded by a formidable belt of rocks and cliffs, among which ranges the haughty promontory of Penninis. You find there all the charms of a green and well-tilled country, watered by streams and rills, and forming a perpetual contrast with the gloomiest landscapes and the wildest beauties. The farms look remarkably prosperous. Cabins, built of stone without mortar, and covered with a thatched roof fastened down by large haybands, serve as granaries to receive the produce of the harvest. The fields are divided by blackberry hedges, along which children, with red hands and teeth, pluck bunches to make pies. The farmers ride or drive. I remember meeting, in one of the sandy, well-kept roads, an old-fashioned coach drawn by two black mares, which seemed to regret that the island was not larger so that they might display their ardour. Near the town, gardens belonging to the inhabitants extend along the side of a hill; it is here that everybody cultivates his vegetables in the evening. Fruit-trees only prosper in spots sheltered from the winds. Near Old Town there is an excellent orchard, surrounded by earth ramparts and walls raised against the enemy of vegetation—that is to say, the sea-breeze. Here flowers, generally found only in greenhouses, mix condescendingly with useful plants. The walls are very rarely bare; they are nearly always covered with a grass called the ice-plant (*Mesunbryanthemum cristallinum*), which is a native of the Cape of Good Hope, and forms delightful hedges. The principal cultivation of the island, however, is the potato, which grows early in warm and sandy soil, and is sent as a dainty to Covent Garden market.

The necessity of building, and making a fortune, is one of the maladies of modern civilization, especially in England. I greatly fear that this malady has crossed the sea, and infected the Scillonians. I stopped in the interior of the island, before a newly-built house, decorated with a certain degree of taste. A pale, thin, worn-out man accosted me and told me its history. "I built that house," he said; "it is very pretty, very pleasant, but it has killed me. In order to procure the means for carrying out my enterprise I condemned myself to live for ten years on potatoes, and work like a horse. The result you can see (and he pointed to his enfeebled limbs). As the house rose and grew better and better, I pined away. Now that is completed, I have only two years to live."

The spot that attracted me most frequently was the churchyard outside the town, on a rough and uneven spot. A wall, clumsily made of rocks, encloses it. I like to read on tombstones the chronicles of localities. The epitaphs told me that the inhabitants of St. Mary's generally attained a fine old age when they were not cut off by chest diseases or disasters at sea. On more than one stone was carved the word "drowned." Such monuments, simple slabs of slate, erect, and turned toward the sea as toward a symbol of eternity, have a rustic and venerable appearance. An old church in a very dilapidated condition, the remains of a larger building half destroyed by the weather, groups these tombs around it with a sort of love—just as the bird collects its eggs in the nest. I saw this cemetery by day, and it was cheerful; I revisited it at night, and it was sinister. The sea-breeze whistled, and sounds ran along the grass as if the dead were talking together. The moon rose slowly behind the rocks, with her glacial, spectral pallor. Everything was silent: the only thing audible was the mighty voice of the ocean, chanting a grave and solemn hymn, resembling a cradle lullaby for those sleeping in the tombs.

CHAPTER XI.

THE ADMIRAL'S GRAVE—THE SHARKS—THE LIGHT-VESSEL AT SEVEN STONES—CHARACTERISTICS OF A LIGHT-VESSEL—THE CHAINS—AN ESCAPED CONVICT—THE CREWS OF THE LIGHT-SHIPS—ONE MONTH ASHORE AND TWO AFLOAT—INSUFFICIENT FOOD—THE ARGAND LAMP—LIFE OF THE MEN ABOARD—A BIRD PIE—DISCIPLINE—THE COST OF A LIGHT-VESSEL.

THE ocean which surrounds the Scilly Isles is an object of terror for mariners. At St. Mary's, in Pothellick Bay, lies what is called the Admiral's Grave. Sir Cloudesley Shovel was returning from Toulon in 1707, when his ship and several others ran on the rocks which form the western group of this chain of granite. He was buried with his dog; and two stones, one at the head, the other at the foot, mark on the bare sand the place of this old sepulchre. But why talk of old shipwrecks? During my stay at the Scilly Isles, a French schooner, the *Dunkerquoise*, entered Port St. Mary's, with its mainmast carried away, its side ripped open, and taking in water at every seam. The sailors were light-haired lads of Brittany, who had been in pursuit of the cod in the chill waters of Iceland. The fishing proved good, but on their return they were run down at night by an English steamer. The crew fortunately escaped on board the steamer, with the exception of a boy fifteen years of age, who was lost and drowned in the catastrophe. His boots and poor clothing were put in a bag; the straw of his bed was thrown into the sea, and all was over. The captain still had tears in his eyes.

Sometimes at St. Mary's, in winter, as many as eight or ten corpses are picked up on the beach and silently carried along the streets. The parade itself has been invaded by the waves during certain winds. After a shipwreck sharks appear in these seas, scenting and pursuing the dead bodies. Such calamities, however, constitute a branch of trade at any rate for the islanders. In winter they make money by collecting the harvest of the tempests. Disasters, it is true, are growing less frequent since the seas have been better lighted; and probably some of the inhabitants of the Scilly Isles feel in their hearts annoyed at this improvement. But what would you? Progress cannot satisfy everybody.

This latter circumstance, the lighting of the seas, reminded me of the object of my voyage. I had come to see the light-ship which in 1841 was anchored about two miles to the east of the Seven Stones, a sombre group of rocks which announce their presence by the circle of foam the sea describes in breaking against them. I was obliged to wait for perfectly calm weather, for the boatmen of St. Mary's will not risk such a trip for any consideration, when the wind blows and the tide is unfavourable. In the boat I was myself able to appreciate the fury of the waves caught in a network of cliffs, and the extraordinary volume of these seas when, on certain days, as the sailors say, ships sink like a lump of lead. We arrived, however, without difficulty, after rounding St. Martin's Head, near Trescau.

At first sight, and from a distance, a light-vessel by day is very like any ordinary ship. If you look at it more closely, you will find a very great difference. The light-ship floats, but it does not move: its short, thick masts have no sails, and are surmounted by large balls; other vessels represent motion, this one immobility. What is usually asked of a ship is to feel the wind and sea: what is asked of the light-ship is that it shall resist the elements. What would happen if, driven by the storm, it should happen to drift? Like a meteor, this wandering beacon would deceive the pilots instead of warning them. A vessel that does not navigate is therefore the ideal which the builder of a light-ship proposes to himself, and this ideal has naturally aroused the imagination of naval architects in various ways. The shape varies according to the localities; the hull of the vessel is larger in Ireland than in England; but in all cases the same object is sought—resistance to the force of the winds and waves. It must ride at anchor with the least possible motion, in the most raging seas and in positions most exposed to the power of the currents.

In order that it should remain at the same spot, it was necessary to attach it. A galley slave, riveted to a chain and iron cables, it cannot move either to the right or left. The length of this chain varies with the localities: at Seven Stones, where the vessel rests on 240 feet of water, it measures a quarter of a mile in length. During the last few years restraints have been added which subjugate the movements of the ship, and also that, though a slave, it should drag as lightly as possible on its chains. There are very few instances of a light-ship having broken its fetters, and not one of a shipwreck; nor have the crew ever been known to alter its position voluntarily, however great the fury of the tempest might be. If, however, the ship is moved by the irresistible force of the elements to such an extent that its light may become a source of error for navigation, a red signal is hoisted, and a gun fired; but it is generally very soon restored to its original position. The danger of drifting, and the presence of mind which the different manœuvres require in such cases, sufficiently display the courage of the men who live all the year round under such a menace. As everything must be foreseen, a spare vessel is held in readiness at the head quarters of the district: the news is soon known by the telegraphs established along the coast, and frequently, before sunset, the spare vessel is towed at full speed, and occupies the place of the one torn away by the tempest. The light-vessels of Trinity House are painted red, those of Ireland are black. It has been found that red and black were the two colours which formed the best contrast with the general colour of the sea. The name of the vessel is painted on its side in large letters. A flag bearing a crown quartered with four ships floats on the breeze; they are the arms of Trinity House.

Two sailors keeping watch on deck saw our boat coming, and made us signs that we could come aboard. The crew of the light-vessel is composed of a master, a mate, and nine men. Among these nine, three attend to the lamps, while the other six, among whom there is a skilful carpenter, maintain order and cleanliness in the light-vessel. We must not, however, expect to find the crew complete; only two-thirds of the sailors are aboard, while their comrades live for a time ashore. Experience has proved that a perpetual stay on board such a ship was beyond the moral and physical forces of human nature. The crushing monotony of the same scenes, the sight of the same waters all white with foam as far as the eye can see, the eternal howling of the breeze, and the thunder of the waves, so deafening that at times the men cannot hear each other speak—all this must have a painful influence on the mind. I forgot the vicinity of the Seven Stones, that stern neighbourhood— ever swallowed up but ever remaining—with its two pointed rocks standing out like tusks at low water.

If there is anything astonishing, it is to find men capable of braving an existence surrounded by such stern conditions: the English themselves have placed the crews of light-vessels among the "curiosities of civilization." In order, however, to mitigate the rigours of such a profession, it has been decided that the sailors should spend two months aboard and one ashore; the master and mate alternate every month. But, even in this case, the ocean must be benignant; for it is not always its good pleasure to allow the men to relieve one another. It frequently happens during the winter that storm and sea oppose every sort of landing, and that weeks elapse before a communication can be re-established between the light-ship and the Scilly Isles. The sailors ashore are employed in cleaning the chains, painting the buoys, filling the oil-tins, or in other tasks of a similar nature. At such times those of the Seven Stones live at Trescau. A very interesting remark for those who occupy themselves with the physiology of dreams was made to me by one of the latter: whenever he was ashore, he told me, he dreamed of the sea; all the time he was afloat he dreamed of land.

On board I admired the neatness of the men and the vessel. What an air of frankness and assurance these weather-beaten faces displayed! Sufficiently contented with their lot, they only complain of the quantity and quality of the rations. The bread allowance (seven pounds a week) is not, according to them, sufficient for hearty men, and I confess from experiment that the sharp air to which they are exposed is well adapted to sharpen the appetite. When they are at sea food is supplied them by Trinity House: ashore they receive fifteen pence a day in lieu of provisions. One of the two lamp-trimmers (the third is ashore) performs the duties of cook for a month. Formerly, if public rumour may be believed, the crews of the light-vessels, isolated by continual storms that rendered the sea impracticable, were reduced to the cruel necessity of dying of hunger. At present a steam-boat or good sailing vessel performs the monthly service with tolerable regularity. In bad weather the communication is never suspended for more than six weeks, and the crew have a sufficient supply of food to last them longer than that time, should it be necessary.

A light-vessel, we must not forget, has two

duties to perform: it must signal a danger, and serve as a torch on the seas. The danger here is the Seven Stones, and the vessel has been placed as near the reef as was safe. As for the system of lighting, it was determined by the conditions in which the light is expected to *live.* However securely a ship may be anchored, it always moves a little with the rising and falling sea. In such a case, it was not possible to use those great fixed lanterns, those massive crystal hives, which are frequently seen in lighthouses. The apparatus consists of Argand lamps, which oscillate in the air till they have attained a vertical position. All this is kept with extreme cleanliness; and the silver reflectors are so well polished that the eye cannot discover the slightest mark on them. The lanterns in which the lamps are fixed surround the mast; they are lowered on to the deck by day to be cleaned and filled with oil; and at night this crown of light is hoisted by a rope. The vessel is also supplied with cannon and a gong: the cannon is fired when ships are seen carelessly approaching the Seven Stones. The gong is a sonorous copper instrument, which is struck during a fog or snow storm to announce the presence of danger. Unfortunately, foreign ships do not always understand these signals.

The crew of the light-vessel have only seen two wrecks on the reef; in the first case they saved one man, in the second, all the passengers excepting a missionary's wife. Saving life is no part of their duty, and the administration admires without encouraging such acts of heroism: their duty is to watch the light, and it is to that alone they have sworn to devote themselves. The discipline is strict, and no man is allowed to leave his post under any pretext. In 1854 a sailor, having heard of the death of his wife, deserted the vessel in order to go to London, where she was to be buried. He was reprimanded; but, in consideration of the motive for which he absented himself, he was not discharged the service. The light-ship of the Seven Stones is the most exposed and menaced of all those along the coast; the master, however, told me that it rides more easily on the long waves than other vessels anchored in a cross sea. According to him, this brave vessel is always eager for the fray; and yet the deck is at times washed by the waves, and when the sea strikes it, the noise resembles the discharge of a four-pounder.

The life of the crew is nearly the same on board all light-vessels. On Sundays, at sunrise, the lantern is lowered; the lamplighter cleans and prepares the lamps for night. At eight o'clock everybody must be up; the hammocks are hung up, and breakfast is served. After this the sailors clean themselves and put on their uniform, of which they are proud, for on the buttons figure the arms of Trinity House. At half-past ten they assemble in the cabin for religious service. At sunset the lighted lantern is hoisted—the true standard of the ship; and then they re-assemble to pray and read the Bible. With the exception of the morning and evening services, the other days of the week are very like Sunday. Wednesdays and Fridays are the grand cleaning days; the vessel must then shine with cleanliness. Looking after and keeping in repair the lamps, keeping watch on deck, noting seven times every twenty-four hours the conditions of the wind and the atmosphere, making sure at the change of the moon that the chains are in good order—such is the almost invariable round of occupations. These tasks, however, leave moments of leisure, which are employed in reading. There is always a library on board, and the works pass from hand to hand. Under such circumstances, who would not pity a man unable to read or write? Such, however, is the condition of the sailors when they enter the service; but, either through the force of example, or the necessity of getting through the crushing wearisomeness of idle hours, it frequently happens that, with the help of the master or mate, they more or less repair the absolute want of education. There is, for instance, one sailor who taught himself sufficiently to become mate, and he is now one of the best officers of the company. The sailors also engage in all sorts of works of patience or fancy; some of them are shoemakers and tailors.

Certain maritime episodes occur now and then to break the fearful monotony of this taciturn existence. In the same way as a lighted candle attracts moths, the light of the ship every now and then attracts clouds of birds in the middle of the night. Some of them fall dead on the deck or stunned by the blow, others cling to the lantern, and are too exhausted to escape the sailors' grasp. It is said that a thousand of these birds were thus captured in one night by the crew of a light-vessel, and that the sailors made out of them a gigantic sea-pie. These sailors receive about £2 15s. a month, which increases as they rise higher. The captain receives £80 a year. They are nearly all married, and fathers. Ashore, they are fond of cultivating a small garden adorned with flowers and vegetables; at sea, they have the feeling of being useful; and this conviction is the basis of the stoical courage with which they support the solitude of the ocean. Their destiny resembles that of the vessel they inhabit during the greater part of the year—chained, obliged to resist the assaults of the waves and winds, chafing the bit as it were—she suffers, but she lights.

The United Kingdom possesses forty-seven floating lights, of which thirty-four belong in England to Trinity House, four in Ireland to the Ballast Board, and the rest to local authorities. Building and fitting up one of these vessels costs from £3,622 to £6,224. The maintenance of each ship, including the oil, wages, clothing and food of the men, entails on Trinity House an annual expense of £1,103. The light-vessels certainly render great services, they are famously adapted to the outline of a part of the British coast, and this circumstance sufficiently explains their invention in England; but these lights cannot be raised to a great power, hence the lighthouse is preferred to them at all the spots where nature has allowed certain works of masonry to be erected.* We must now study this second branch of lighting of the seas.

* Without even leaving the Scilly Isles, two very interesting lighthouses can be visited, that of St. Agnes and that of Bishop's Rock. The latter succeeded an edifice which was blown down by a violent storm in 1850. It stands on an isolated rock in the middle of the sea, and is so difficult of access that the keepers of the lighthouse never venture to approach it without life-belts on. They have to leap out of the boat on to a rock as polished as a diamond, and if the foot slip or the hand fail to clutch the angles of the rock, the man is hurled into the sea. This lighthouse, one of the most admirable works in stone, and the most exposed to the assaults of the waves, was struck in 1860 by a waterspout, which carried off its bell, hung 100 feet above the ordinary high-water level. Fresh meat and vegetables will not keep there; and hence the men are at times attacked by scurvy. Ashore, they live at St. Mary's, in neat white cottages placed at their disposal by Trinity House.

CHAPTER XII.

THREE SYSTEMS OF LIGHTHOUSES—PLYMOUTH BREAKWATER—FOG-SIGNALS—THE BELL AND THE SEA-GULLS—THE STORY OF EDDYSTONE LIGHTHOUSE—HENRY WINSTANLEY—JOHN RUDIERD—THE LIGHTHOUSE ON FIRE—SMEATON—A TREE OF STONE—EXTERIOR AND INTERIOR OF EDDYSTONE LIGHTHOUSE—ITS APPEARANCE DURING A STORM—THE LIGHTHOUSE NOW KEPT BY THREE MEN—LIFE OF THE KEEPERS—A COBBLER SHUT UP THROUGH HATRED OF CAPTIVITY—LONGSHIP'S LIGHTHOUSE AND THE ROARING CAVERNS—A SILENT LIGHT-KEEPER—THE SMALLS AND WHITESIDE—DANGER OF STARVATION—THE DOUBLE STANNERS LIGHT—POINT OF HONOUR AMONG THE KEEPERS—BELL ROCK LIGHTHOUSE—ROBERT STEPHENSON—THE SKERRYVORE LIGHTHOUSE—ALAN STEPHENSON—SYSTEMS OF LIGHTING—AUTHORITY AND LIBERTY.

THE lighthouses, or buildings intended to serve as vehicles for light, are built on three entirely different systems in England. The first are mounted on tall scaffoldings at the mouths of tidal rivers, and bear some likeness to beacons. This scaffolding is of wood or iron bars, and supports the main building in the air, so that the waves may dash and foam for centuries without reaching the top in which the light *lives*. The solidity of such curious buildings generally contradicts the proverb which says that houses built on sand are unable to defy the shock of the wind and waters. The second lighthouses are towers which rise with much greater dignity on the coast. Surrounded by white cottages, and enclosed by a wall, they face the sea which they command. A fine specimen of these lighthouses may be seen at Lizard Cape. The building consists of two towers surmounted by a lantern, and connected by a covered gallery, so that the keeper may pass from one to the other during the night without being exposed to the rain or blast. The offices, store-rooms, and keepers' houses form, with the tower, a mass of whitewashed buildings which, owing to its striking colour, forms a landmark for sailors by day. Lastly, the third lighthouses are granite giants, erect and isolated amid the ocean. They might be compared to Prometheus: nailed to the rock, they raise their arms to Heaven, as if defying Jupiter, and hold aloft the fire which all the fury of the tempest cannot extinguish. The erection of this last system of lighthouses is evidently the triumph of architecture applied to the science of engineering. The oldest of these is the one which rises in the midst of the sea on Eddystone Rock.

I set out from Sutton Port, the old port of Plymouth, in a stout boat managed by two men; it was eight in the morning, and I was warned that the voyage there and back would last nearly the whole day. We passed in front of the citadel, where circular batteries were being built on the naked, grim hills. On arriving in Plymouth Channel, we noticed on our right the Breakwater, a Titanic work. It is a road paved with granite, and running for a mile into the sea, whose savage impetuosity it breaks. The first stone—an enormous block—was laid, or, to speak more correctly, cast into these waters on April 12th, 1812. Since then quarries of four million tons of rock have been thrown in to fill the ocean bed at this spot. I stopped at the Breakwater, as I was curious not only to inspect this stupendous barrier which subdues the fury of the waves, but also a lighthouse, built in 1843, which stands at the western extremity of the Breakwater. After walking for some time over slabs of granite, I found, at the end of this Cyclopean road, a grey tower, pierced with narrow irregular windows, crowned by a lantern, and flanked by a smoking chimney-pot. The door, which is massive, and set in a framework of iron, is reached by climbing up some granite steps as steep as the rounds of a ladder; it was evidently desired to close the entrance of the tower against a dangerous visitor, and this visitor is the sea, which in rough weather at times rises to the top of the breakwater, which is, however, eighteen or twenty feet above the low-water mark. Inside, a winding staircase, such as is found in old castles, leads, first, to the oil-room, where there are six large cisterns. Next come the store-room, the bed-room, the dwelling-room, and the watch-room. The whole is surmounted by a glass cage, covered by a roof also of glass, in the centre of which is the lantern, eight feet high, and supported by bronze pillars. This lantern is provided with four reflectors, and 118 mirrors; the light reaches a distance of eight miles; it is red to those who see it from the sea, and white to those observing it from the coast. To the lighthouse is attached a bell, which is constantly rung in foggy weather; and such is the experience of the pilots, that, according as the sound of this bell reaches them, they know at once in what part of the sea they are. The best system for a fog-signal is not yet decided. There is at least one preferable to the bell. In the South Stack Lighthouse, near Holyhead, built on the middle of an island under a cliff, and connected with the mainland by a bridge, tamed sea-birds are employed. The gulls perch on the walls of the lighthouse, and utter cries that warn the sailors. This lighthouse has a bell and a gun; but the natural signal has been judged so superior that the cannon has been removed some distance from the rock, for fear lest the noise might startle the birds. In this island the young gulls run about among the white rabbits, with which they live on intimate terms.

The staff consists of three men, who each pass

two months in the lighthouse and one month on shore. The two who are on duty relieve one another during the night. They receive their provisions once a month from Plymouth, consisting chiefly of dried vegetables and salt meat. In case of one of the men being taken ill, the telegraph is set to work, and if it is at night, the signal is given with a light. Their wives and children are allowed to visit them in a boat by day, but must leave the place at sunset. During winter the waves often rise above the roof of the tower. These two lighthouses—that of the Breakwater and the Eddystone—have some connection together, in so far as being on the same route, they guide vessels desiring to enter Plymouth Harbour by night from one light to the other. There is, however, a difference between them—as between a dwarf and a giant. My boat, which had been momentarily fastened to the iron rings of the breakwater, was now about to convey me to the colossus.

The story of Eddystone lighthouse has been told with noble simplicity by the man who had the glory of building it. A first undertaker, Henry Winstanley, built, in 1696, on this rock isolated in the sea, a house which bore some resemblance to a Chinese pagoda or a belvidere. An engraving of the day, executed by the architect's orders, represents him as indulging in the innocent sport of angling out of a window.

This house, loaded with devices and inscriptions, crowned with open galleries, bristling with angles, corners, and fanciful ornaments, had in reality but one fault—it was not solid. This Henry Winstanley appears to have been an eccentric. After erecting a building which left much to be desired as regarded strength and stability, he incessantly called on the tempest with an air of triumph and defiance. "Blow, winds," he was heard shouting, in an attack of lyrical boldness, "revolt, sea; unchain yourselves, ye elements, and come and try my work." The tempest came as requested, but it was to swallow up the building and the architect. On November 26th, 1703, Winstanley had gone to the rock to effect some repairs to the lighthouse, and during the night an awful storm tore away the building with its inhabitants, and only left an iron chain riveted into the stone.

Still, a lighthouse was necessary on the Eddystone. Since the light had been extinct, a man-of-war, the *Winchelsea*, perished by running on this bank, and more than half the crew were lost. The difficulty of the enterprise did not discourage John Rudierd, a London mercer, who kept a shop on Ludgate Hill. Accident had made a tradesman of him, but Nature impelled him to be an engineer. In July, 1706, he set to work and succeeded in building a wooden tower, which excited the admiration of the most competent judges. The new light was inaugurated in July,

1708, and for forty-seven years it did not cease to flame and be a guide to ships. Rough winters succeeded each other; the waves rose furiously; the tempests—even that of 1744, which left many sad memories—passed over the building without destroying it. This second lighthouse resisted the power of the water, but was destroyed by fire. Early on the night of December 1st, 1755, a dark winter's night, everything was quiet in the tower, when about two A.M. the keeper on duty went as usual into the lantern to snuff the candles, and found it full of smoke. He had scarce opened the door when the draught made the flames burst forth. This keeper, who was an old man, alarmed his two comrades; but the latter were asleep, and some time elapsed ere they came to his help. While waiting for them, he tried to put out the fire with a water-pipe placed on the upper floor; but his efforts were in vain. A shower of molten lead fell from the top of the tower on his head, his shoulders, and even down his throat.* The two other keepers were equally unsuccessful; the supply of water was exhausted, and to renew it they must descend and ascend a flight of seventy stairs. There was no other prospect but to beat a retreat. They retired from storey to storey before the fire, which pursued them to the very edge of the sea. For-

---

* This man, old Hall, died twelve days after the fire, and the physicians found a piece of lead in his stomach.

tunately the tide was low, and they were thus enabled to find refuge under a chain of rocks that rises to the east of the Eddystone. Toward daybreak, the livid reflection of the fire was seen by the fishermen of Cawsand and Ram Head, who arrived with their boats; but at this hour the tide was high and the breeze freshening; hence, then, some difficulty in helping the three trembling light-keepers, who seemed struck with stupor. Such was the fate of the second lighthouse built on Eddystone Rock.

It was reserved for Smeaton, a mathematical instrument maker, to conquer by science and calculation the obstinate resistance of the conspiring elements. Warned, but not discouraged, by the failure of his two predecessors, he resolved to erect a stone tower. His edifice might be defined as a granite tree rooted in the rock. It was from observing nature, he tells us himself, from considering the trunk of an oak, that he conceived the idea of a monument destined to brave by its form, as well as the solidity of its material, the frightful violence of the tempest. The first stone was laid June 15th, 1757, and the last August 24th, 1759. This third lighthouse is the one I now saw rising sadly and proudly from the depth of the ocean. With each puff of wind that bore us nearer it seemed to grow larger, and I was then better able to comprehend the etymology of the name given to the Eddystone. Standing in the midst of this circle of foam, the lighthouse rises, painted in alternate bands of red and white: these two colours are well adapted to catch the eye of sailors.* When we landed we scaled rough steps cut in the rock, and found ourselves at the base of the tower, with our faces turned toward the sea, which angrily surrounded us. The two boatmen who brought me waved their round hats in the direction of Plymouth, which is about fifteen miles distant.

On examining the characteristics of the building close at hand, the solidity of this tower can be properly appreciated; it only forms, as it were, a single stone, so closely are the dovetailed pieces of granite blended with each other. The internal arrangements greatly resemble those of all lighthouses, being composed of a kitchen, two store-rooms, a bed-room, and a lantern. On the granite cornice running round the second store-room are the following words, which have never

* To comprehend the importance attaching to the colour of lighthouses, it must be borne in mind that these buildings answer two purposes: at night they light, and by day act as a landmark for sailors. In the latter case, they cannot be too visible. The natural colour of the stone or granite does not at all suit them; it is too blended with the colour of the rocks, and does not stand out sufficiently against the sky. Curious experiments have been made on this point. Sportsmen who pursue wild birds on the sea-shore have seen that birds of a dark colour can be more easily kept in sight, and that young swans, owing to their greyish hue, were the most difficult of all to distinguish. Taking advantage of this hint of nature, the coast-guardsmen, who require to conceal themselves from the sea, surround themselves with white and grey colours.

been used more appropriately: "Except the Lord build the house, their labour is but vain who build it." On the last stone of the edifice, above the door of the lantern, the joyous and grateful architect inscribed *Laus Deo.* Formerly this lantern was lighted with candles; but in 1807, when the Eddystone was given over to Trinity House, lamps, with parabolic reflectors of silvered copper, were substituted for this old system. At a distance of thirteen miles this light has a brilliancy equal to that of the brightest star in Ursa Major. There is a gallery at the top of the tower, from which the immensity of the ocean can be surveyed.

As it has to support the shock of the Atlantic and the Bay of Biscay, this building has been more than once exposed to terrible trials. In heavy weather, the multitude of irritated waves rushes against the sides of the tower. This column of water, in breaking, bounds over the roof of the building, and then falls back in cataracts of formidable weight. Covered with a helm of foam, or enveloped in a transparent spray, the lighthouse then resembles at a distance a model placed under a glass. Some one told Smeaton that if the tower resisted the furious tempest which broke out early in 1762, it would last to the day of judgment. I know not how this will be, but Eddystone lighthouse braved this storm, and many others, without wincing. During these turmoils, the men felt the edifice tremble and vibrate like the stem of a mighty oak shaken by the hurricane. Is this an effect of what Smeaton himself calls the elasticity of stone?

At the beginning, this lighthouse was the scene of a dark tragedy. It was then kept by two men who relieved each other to keep watch and put up fresh candles. One day a signal of distress was seen flying from the tower. The system of signalling was not greatly developed at that time, and moreover the sea was so bad that boats could not approach near enough to speak to the keepers of the lighthouse. What was going on inside? The most alarming conjectures ran along the coast, but yet at nightfall the light still burned. The two keepers had mothers; they were married, and great was the anxiety of the poor women. At last, though the weather was still alarming, sailors were able to land on the reef with some difficulty. A revolting smell filled the whole tower, and at once announced the presence of a corpse. Only one man was alive, and what that man had suffered could be guessed from his pallor, his gloomy silence, and his thin and enfeebled limbs. His comrade had been dead for nearly a month : his first idea was to cast the body into the sea. When about to do so, he was restrained by a frightful reflection that crossed his brain like a flash. Would he not be accused of being an assassin? Would not the human law cry in his ears, "Cain, what hast thou done with thy brother?" In these silent abodes, where a crime could be so easily committed, what witnesses could he call to his justification? The stones, the dark waves, the voiceless walls of this solitary tower, rose, on the contrary, to accuse him. Struck with terror, he consequently resigned himself to live with the dead man. A cooper by trade, he made a clumsy coffin in which he laid his comrade; then, with sublime courage, he alone undertook to watch the light. Because a man was dead, ships must not be exposed to the risk of running on the rocks and being wrecked. Hence the light still shone! The supernatural efforts the wretched man imposed on himself alone in the tower, and, as it were, in the presence of death, destroyed his constitution. When the sailors found these two men—one already decomposed, the other haggard and livid—they fancied they saw a corpse guarded by a ghost. From this time three men have been always employed in lighthouses isolated in the sea.

The life of the keepers is rather monotonous. The wind blows sometimes with such violence that they can hardly breathe. They are then obliged to shut themselves up closely in the tower, darkened by a gloomy fog or by the spray of the lofty waves, which envelopes them like a rent veil. There they listen for hours to the voice of the angry waves, expecting nothing from man, and only trusting in God. On fine days in summer they go on to the rock at ebb tide and amuse themselves with fishing. Though this existence is so slightly varied, it however finds partisans. A man had lived forty years in Eddystone lighthouse, and conceived such an attachment for his prison, that during two summers he gave up his term of leave to his comrades. He wished to do the same the third year, but was so urged, that he at length consented this time to profit by his claim. As long as he had been on the rock and in his stone dungeon, he had behaved well—ashore he found himself in a strange land, and, doubtless, to drown his grief, gave way to habits of intoxication. He was taken back in that state to Eddystone lighthouse, in the hope that he would recover his senses and temperate habits there. After languishing for some days he died.

Smeaton mentions another instance, which will explain the thoughts of some of the employés. A cobbler engaged himself as lamplighter at the Eddystone. During the passage, the coxswain of the boat asked him, "How is it, Master Jacob, that you are going to shut yourself up there, when ashore you could earn half-a-crown or three shillings a day, while a light-keeper only receives ten shillings a week?" "Every man to his liking," Jacob answered; "I was always fond of independence." The remark is not without truth, though it may appear so strange when applied to a life of seclusion and a sort of cellular regimen. What really constitutes a prison is the moral captivity. Here, on the contrary, the mind is free; it soars over the savage steppes of the ocean, all studded with sails. To confine a man by force under such conditions would seem almost a legal barbarity; but from the moment that the choice is voluntary, and this isolation is a favour instead of a punishment, the gloomy dungeon itself is robbed of half its rigour by losing the idea of slavery.

There are natures, however, that cannot resist the crushing uniformity of the same scenes and the same external impressions. About a mile and a quarter from the Land's End, on a group of granite isles surrounded by the sea, there stands a lighthouse, built in 1793, which is called the Longship's. The conical rock on which it stands is the Carn-Brás, which emerges forty-five feet above the level of low water. In winter, the rock and the building at times disappear for some seconds behind the waves, which mount some fathoms above the lantern. One day, the sea carried away the cap of this lantern; the water entered, extinguished the lamps, and was taken out with great difficulty. Another circumstance heightens the terror of the spot. There is beneath the lighthouse a cavern. When the sea is rough, the noise produced by the air compressed in this cavern is so violent that the men can hardly speak. One of them was struck with such fear by this natural phenomenon, that his hair turned white in a night. Other roaring caverns exist at the Lizard and in Scotland.

Though this situation is so melancholy, there are some persons who like it, for one of the lamplighters lived in this tower for nineteen years. One day, however, in 1862, two black flags floated from the top of the lighthouse; it was evidently a distress signal. What had happened? Of the three men who inhabited the tower, the one whose turn of duty it was had stabbed himself with a knife. His companions had tried to stanch the blood by thrusting tow into the wound. Three days had thus passed ere help could be obtained. The sea was so rough and landing so dangerous, that they were obliged to place the wounded man in a sort of hammock in the lighthouse boat. He was attended to, but died shortly after he reached the shore. The jury, after hearing the evidence of his comrades, gave a verdict of temporary insanity. It is not surprising that a man placed under such frightful circumstances should feel the dizziness of the deep rise to his brain.

What adds greatly to the horrors of this imprisonment in the midst of the waves is the forced intercourse between men whose tastes and tempers do not always agree. Some visitors having landed at the Eddystone one day, they remarked to one of the keepers how happy he must feel in this retirement. "Yes, very happy," the lightkeeper answered, "if we could only enjoy the pleasure of conversation; but for a whole month my mate and I have not exchanged a word." Now that they are three, they have a better chance of talking; but the perpetual friction between these angular characters, joined to a common domicile and the annoyance of captivity, at times engenders deep aversions. Not so very long ago, the administration were obliged to interpose between two keepers who could not endure one another. It discharged one of them, as the only way of settling the affair.

The material condition of the lightkeepers has been greatly ameliorated since they have been attached to Trinity House. Before that period the most heartrending calamities frequently took place in the lighthouses. One day some people on the beach picked up on the sand what the English call a message from the deep; that is to say, a letter placed in a carefully-sealed bottle, which in its turn was enclosed in a barrel. On the barrel were inscribed the words, "Open this, and you will find a letter." This sad message came from a group of rocks—the Smalls—situated in the middle of the sea off Skomer Island, to the south of Wales. On this group of reefs, a young man of the name of Whiteside, a musical instrument maker by trade, but whom Nature had endowed with a singular genius for great enterprises, aided by a band of Cornish miners and one or two shipbuilders, had succeeded in building a lighthouse. Who can say what dangers they incurred, what heroic courage they displayed, in this obstinate struggle against the elements? And now, this same Whiteside, abandoned and forgotten, was exposed to a death by starvation in the trembling house which he had, so to speak, conquered from the waves. Many other mournful stories are told. Light-keepers, deprived of every other resource, have been reduced, if we may believe tradition, to drink the oil and eat the candles. Even in that they were obliged to be temperate, for before all they must think about feeding the light.

Fire is the soul of the lighthouse, and to the maintenance of this fire the lightkeepers consecrate themselves with the devotion of vestal virgins. Whatever may happen, and no matter what weather, the lantern must shine at all hours of the night and on every night of the year. "You will light your lamps every night at sunset, and keep them bright and clear till sunrise." Such is their first commandment, and it contains all the law and the prophets. This lighthouse slave must be at his post on the rock like a planet in the sky. On this condition, but only on this condition, the men will be decently paid, well fed, and clothed; they will receive in their old days a pension, which, in some cases, extends to their widows—an insurance on their lives which will keep their families from want. They will be supplied with books and medicines; certain principles of morality, order, and cleanliness will be inculcated in them, which they can transmit to their wives and children: but before all, they must not forget the light. Like the flag in a redoubt, it is the last thing they must abandon after a defeat.

Two or three years ago a lighthouse which at that time stood on a point called the Double Stanners, between Lytham and Blackpool, had been threatening to collapse for some time past, owing to the invasions of the waves, which gradually wash away the coast at that spot. Workmen laboured in vain to fortify the building, by raising fresh pillars round its base and strengthening the part that faced the sea. The keepers noticed one night that the tower was vibrating more than usual. The next morning they discovered that a portion of the front had fallen down, and that nearly all the foundation was undermined by the sea. They removed their furniture, but left the necessary implements to light the lamps. At nightfall, the high tide surrounded them, the wind blew with such violence that there was very little hope of the building holding out till morning, but still the light had never shone more brilliantly than on that night. On the next day a gust levelled the lighthouse, but the men retired with all the honours of war; the fire had burned till the last moment.

I should have liked to have passed the night in Eddystone lighthouse; but, unfortunately for me, this is a favour never granted to any one. It is feared that strangers may disturb the men on their duty, or interrupt the light by walking on the lantern gallery. Besides, what should I have seen? Apparitions of ships gliding over the dark sea, the merry faces of sailors looking toward the coast, and which, momentarily illumined, would have disappeared in the immensity of the night. Hence I left the Eddystone before sunset, and, tossed by the waves, quietly returned to Plymouth, though not without looking back several times at the lighthouse, which was diminishing in the horizon.

This Herculean task was greatly surpassed sixty years ago. Smeaton was followed by giants along the road he had opened. In the Scottish seas, at a distance of a dozen miles from the nearest islands, rises an isolated rock, which had been for centuries an object of terror to sailors. The abbots of Aberbrothwick, who lived in the neighbourhood, had mounted on this reef a huge bell, which the motion of the waves caused to ring constantly, but principally in tempestuous weather. This reef, first called the Inch Cape, afterwards assumed the name of the Bell Rock. This mode of signalling was not very successful; wrecks succeeded wrecks; a man-of-war among others, the *York,* perished with the whole crew. The northern commissioners at length resolved to build a lighthouse on the same principle as the Eddystone, and appointed an engineer, Robert Stephenson, to direct the works. Stephenson landed on the desolate rock with his labourers on August 17th, 1807; but as the reef was covered with twelve feet of water at high tide, the men could only work for a few hours between ebb and flow. One day the engineer and thirty-two masons were nearly drowned by the sea, which suddenly rose; the ship broke its chains and drifted away; another boat was expected, but did not arrive. Robert Stephenson tried to address the terror-stricken group, but his tongue adhered to his palate. He stooped to wash his mouth out in a small puddle of sea-water which was on the rock, when he heard the joyous cry raised around him: "A boat, a boat!"

The tower was finished in October, 1810. Wide at the base, it grows smaller as it rises, exactly like a tree. An iron pier facilitates landing. A bronze ladder attached to the granite column leads to the door, which is a great height above the ground. The keepers declare that the sea at times rises thirteen feet above the base of the building. This lighthouse contains six rooms, and also possesses two powerful bells, which ring during fogs. In the sitting-room is a bust of Robert Stephenson. The four keepers of the Bell Rock lighthouse are married, and have from three to seven children a piece. What must family life be with men thus separated from their domestic hearths for the greater part of the year by all the wrath of the ocean? Byron says that absence makes the heart grow fonder. I myself saw a young woman lately married to a lighthouse-keeper scale dangerous rocks every night in order to watch the distant light. This done, she returned home with a lighter heart: all was right, as the lamp was burning, and wished her a good night.

Another deep-sea lamp-post is Skerryvore lighthouse, the boldest of all the works raised against the powers of the deep. The Skerryvore (great rock) forms the centre of a group of rocks cast into the Atlantic, between the western isles of Scotland and the north of Scotland. In ordinary tides only the point of these reefs is seen, against which the whole force of the waves breaks with an awful din. Still, it was on this inhospitable rock that Alan Stephenson, son of Robert, undertook in 1838 to plant a lighthouse. The first works were carried away by a tempest on the night of September 3rd, 1838. Fresh wooden huts were erected, in which the architect and his thirty men perched themselves forty feet above the rock, which was most usually covered by the furious waves. How many days and nights passed away slowly in these sad aërial abodes! The sea did not even permit the prisoners to descend upon the reef. With what anxiety they watched the coast whence provisions were to come! How relieved they felt after a change of weather sufficiently favourable for them to resume their task! Though their abode was perched so high, they were aroused more than once in the night by terrible shocks: the sea had made a bound, and fell on their roof; the house trembled on its pillars, the water entered by the doors and windows; on two occasions the alarm was so great that the men jumped out of bed.

On July 21st, 1842, however, Alan Stephenson had succeeded in fastening on the rock a granite tower 137 feet high, and in February, 1844, a light burned for the first time on the gloomy group of the Skerryvores. This edifice forms a block of masonry four times larger than the Eddystone lighthouse. The erection of a lighthouse under such circumstances is the most striking and glorious feature of British architecture. The ages of chivalry are not extinct; but the heroes are now-a-days the engineers and workmen, who, with a strength of mind greatly superior to military courage, wage war with the elements in order to bring man nearer to man by extending the relations of navigation and commerce. The ocean itself seems to admire these audacious works, and is tempted to cry with the poet: "Great I must call them, for they conquered me."

A commission appointed to inspect the lights, buoys, and beacons of Great Britain, published in 1861 a voluminous report on the results of the inquiry. The members of this commission performed their task conscientiously; they went all round the United Kingdom, visited the Channel isles, and even the coasts of France and Spain. On their way they examined 1,184 witnesses, and procured official information from thirteen foreign governments. The state of the apparatus intended to produce the light naturally attracted their attention. All sorts of lighting materials were formerly used in the British lighthouses, and the last coal fire, that of St. Rus, was not put out till 1822. Oil is now the sole source of light; but there is great diversity in the use of this combustible. Among the lights, some are fixed, others are revolving lights, appearing, disappearing, and reappearing before sailors like an intermittent star. A great difference also prevails in the arrangement of the lamps. The colours vary and pass through all the hues of the prism, being by turns white, red, green, or blue. Two systems, known by the names of the catoptric and dioptric, add brilliancy and range to the light, either by reflectors or large glass lenses. Of these two systems, the first and elder one has been, however, generally dethroned: the apparatus in the majority of lighthouses now consists of a central flame covered by an enormous crystal bell, which at times costs as much as £1,000. Gas, and the electric light have also been tried with more or less success. The truth is, that lighting the sea is in England, as everywhere else, in a state of transition. Trinity House has engaged the services of Professor Faraday to guide it on the track of modern discoveries.

Another circumstance struck the members of the commission: this is the absence of unity in the system. Out of 357 lighthouses which the United Kingdom possesses, 197 belong to the three great societies of England, Scotland, and Ireland, and 160 to local authorities. Who could expect that perfect harmony would issue from such a division of power? In France, as is well known, things are managed very differently. The lights are lit and put out at the same hour of the day, as if governed by the breath of a central organization. The volume of light, the quantity of oil to be burned every hour to feed the flame, and the most trifling details are regulated with military precision. It might be said that all the springs of the system are worked by the same hand.

This *fiat lux* by authority appears for a

moment to have silenced the members of the British Commission. They wished that such order might be introduced on the other side of the Channel. Their advice, however, has hitherto found but slight echo among a people too jealous of their rights not to reserve the duty of managing their own affairs. Liberty is sometimes mistaken, for she is the daughter of Humanity, and she can always correct and redress her errors; but once lost, how is she to be regained? The English, besides, have a right to be proud of what they have done from generation to generation to light their coasts. Without asking anything of Government, they have built at the wildest spots glorious edifices, real temples of the seas, which cost them from £3,000 up to £80,000 a piece. Every day in the year, at sunset, they raise in their free and invisible arms 404 torches, including the light-vessels, which point out to sailors the snares of the ocean, and unite beneath their light the radiant symbol of the peace and fraternity of nations sailing from every quarter of the globe.

THE END.

www.ingramcontent.com/pod-product-compliance
Lightning Source LLC
Chambersburg PA
CBHW022048230426
43672CB00008B/1101